DATE DUE

MRO 3 '95			
NO 5'96			
OC 23 '98			

FREUD'S CONCEPT OF REPRESSION AND DEFENSE, ITS THEORETICAL AND OBSERVATIONAL LANGUAGE

by Peter Madison

UNIVERSITY OF MINNESOTA PRESS, Minneapolis

PERMISSION to use the extensive quotations herein from the Standard Edition
of Sigmund Freud's work and from his *Collected Papers* was granted by
Anna Freud, Ernst Freud, and the Hogarth Press, London. Publishers of the
following volumes also permitted use of quotations: *A General Introduction
to Psychoanalysis* by Sigmund Freud, by permission of Liveright, Publishers,
New York; *Introductory Lectures on Psychoanalysis* by Sigmund Freud,
translated by Joan Riviere, by permission of George Allen and Unwin, Ltd.,
London; *The Origins of Psychoanalysis* by Sigmund Freud, by permission of
Basic Books, Inc., New York; *New Introductory Lectures on Psychoanalysis*
and *An Outline of Psychoanalysis* by Sigmund Freud, by permission of
W. W. Norton and Co., New York; *Moses and Monotheism* by Sigmund
Freud, by permission of Alfred A. Knopf, New York; *Psychoanalysis, Scientific Method, and Philosophy* edited by Sidney Hook, by permission of New
York University Press, New York; *The Assessment of Human Motives* edited
by Gardner Lindzey, by permission of Holt, Rinehart and Winston, Inc.

TO
Robert Winthrop White

✕. Acknowledgments

THIS study of Freud's theory of repression and defense was made possible through the support of several organizations and many persons. A research grant from the Donner Foundation to the Institute of the Pennsylvania Hospital of Philadelphia provided the initial impetus and financial support. In addition, research funds from the Pennsylvania Hospital Division of the Hall-Mercer Hospital as well as other resources of the Institute of the Pennsylvania Hospital have made it possible for me to complete the book. Some of the writing was done as a part-time staff member of the University of Pennsylvania Medical School, and some while on leave from Swarthmore College. The Faculty Research Fund of the college also provided stenographic help at several points.

I am grateful, particularly, to Dr. Per-Olof Therman, research director of the Institute of the Pennsylvania Hospital, whose belief that psychiatry and psychology need one another led to a fruitful and stimulating association, and to Dr. Lauren H. Smith, who, as administrator-in-chief of the hospital, provided such splendid conditions for work.

A special debt is owed to several champions who were willing to cross the political boundaries between psychology and psychoanalysis to encourage work that fell in the no man's land between. Without such support from Dr. Robert W. White, chairman of the Department of Social Relations at Harvard, and, later, from an anonymous consultant of the University of Minnesota Press, this study would have fallen prey to the many forces within each profession that make the work of a psychologist in the alien territory of psychoanalysis a hazardous venture.

Richard Crutchfield's close reading of the manuscript resulted in many helpful suggestions, and my colleagues in psychology and philosophy at

Swarthmore, as well as Dr. Leon Saul's research seminar group at the University of Pennsylvania Medical School, offered constructive comments at several points in my formulations. Everett Hunt of Swarthmore helped greatly with the style of the manuscript, and my wife, Karlene, has typed and retyped it with patient care. My gratitude goes also to the staff of the University of Minnesota Press.

The generosity of Anna Freud and Ernst Freud and the Hogarth Press of London in allowing the extensive quotations from the Standard Edition of the works of Sigmund Freud and his *Collected Papers* deserves a very special acknowledgment. I am also grateful to the Liveright Publishing Company, George Allen and Unwin, Ltd., Basic Books, Inc., W. W. Norton and Company, Alfred A. Knopf, New York University Press, and Holt, Rinehart and Winston, Inc., for permission to quote from publications of theirs.

PETER MADISON

Princeton University
April 15, 1961

✗. Contents

Freud's Theory of Repression and Defense, Its Theoretical and Observational Language

✗. Introduction

I HAD no intention of writing a book on Freud's theory of repression and defense when I accepted the invitation of the Institute of the Pennsylvania Hospital to spend a summer with their psychiatric staff. It was to be a friendly exchange of ideas in which I was left free to make whatever contributions a psychologist could to their discussions, which at that time were largely concerned with problems in the evaluation of therapy.

The resulting contacts were both stimulating and surprising. Like most academic psychologists, I was unaware of how psychoanalytic psychiatry had become — a situation I soon found to be a national phenomenon. The coolness of a Meyerian age toward Freud had given way to not only a sweeping acceptance of psychoanalysis but even a domination by it. The young resident today is as likely as not to be completing requirements for training as an analyst at a psychoanalytic institute while carrying on his residency program in psychiatry.

My academic orientation was also jolted to find that Freud is not history, as psychologists are accustomed to treat him. In the universities we tend to feel that his ideas have been replaced by neo-Freudians and post-Freudians. I had a difficult time defending my enthusiasm for what I had taken to be new theories in the face of the sophisticated knowledge of Freud that my associates in psychiatry had, and, in the end, I had to concede that ideas in new dress are not necessarily new concepts.

The problem of evaluating psychotherapy proved to be a challenging one. It was also disturbing. The fact that no one, today, can say surely whether one form of therapy is better than another, or better than no therapy, is unsettling to a psychologist reared in the tradition that what-

3

ever exists can be measured. In the records of therapy that we reviewed, psychoanalysts simply reported their results in terms such as "cured," "better," "no change," or "worse." They used a framework of ideas contributed by Freud as working hypotheses in seeking to understand a patient's condition, and in guiding treatment, but then abandoned this theory when it came to evaluating their own efforts.

Herein, it seemed to me, lay the key to better evaluation of therapy. Measures were needed. And, after all, measures are no more than the counting of events that theories point to. A good theory is related to observable events by its correspondence rules or operational definitions, and measures can be devised for such observables. In principle there seemed to be no reason why this would not be true of psychoanalysis. If a theory of illness and cure could be used to indicate what should be counted, measuring therapeutic outcomes ought to be possible in terms springing directly from the theory — there was surely no need to abandon it at the final point.

It did not take long for me to discover that the principal Freudian concept on which everything turns in psychiatry holds that mental illness is a result of defense against anxiety. The patient's condition at the outset is described in terms of his defensive responses, or "repressions," and the cure, obviously, should be stated in the same terms — measures of the outcomes of therapy have to be formulated in terms of repression and defense if they are to be based on theory rather than on everyday judgments of "better" or "worse."

Can repression and defense be measured? I consulted our research literature. Repression, particularly, had been the subject of numerous investigations by psychologists over the years, and some way of measuring it was always under consideration in their studies. But, while these investigations were often conceived as tests of Freud's theory, his theory, or any theory, was rarely discussed. The investigators themselves seemed very uncertain about exactly what they were trying to measure. They seemed to feel that their research was somehow related to repression as seen in the clinic, but even they could not say just what this relationship was. And the findings were contradictory. After much pondering of this bewildering literature, I felt honestly puzzled and unable to say whether anyone had measured repression.

The discrepancy between these laboratory analogues of repression and the day-to-day work of my friends in psychiatry was disconcerting. Al-

4

though precise definitions were notably lacking, psychologists seemed generally to interpret "repression" simply as unconsciously motivated forgetting, while in the clinic "repression" apparently referred to complex processes of which amnesic forgetting was only a small part. The critical emotional situations of clinic patients made the ego-insult techniques of the laboratory analogues look pale and motivationally thin; the forgetting of insults or shock-associated nonsense syllables seemed a far cry from the tragically disturbed lives that were the object of the therapist's study. If repression was to be measured in a way that was relevant to therapy, these past studies by psychologists, interesting as they were in their own right, could offer little help.

The problem at least seemed clearer. It lay in the definition of what was to be measured. If repression was not merely amnesia, this oversimplification had to be abandoned by psychologists and the full meaning recognized before they could contribute to the development of measures. But persistent discussion with my colleagues in psychiatry and reading in the current literature on the psychoanalytic conception of mental illness led to a discovery that astonished me. While psychiatrists clearly used the word "repression" to refer to more than motivated forgetting, just what it meant proved to be very complicated for anyone to state; they had as much difficulty with definition as psychologists. Clinicians took refuge in citing ready clinical examples and pleaded that they were not theorists. The theorists, when they were pinned down, tended to quote Freud.

It was inevitable that, finally, I should turn to Freud's writings. The fact is, as I now appreciate, that there is no theory of personality in psychiatry genuinely independent of Freud's work. Those who have come after him have kept within the framework he set down. The changes are mostly minor and are principally omissions of the more complex parts of his thinking, or a rephrasing of his pseudo-biological terminology in another language, which, on close study, typically shows little gain in precision. It may be pleasanter to speak of "neurotic trends" rather than "pregenital fixations," or "emotional forces" rather than "instincts," but the gain seems more an aesthetic refinement than an advance in theory. Calling the Oedipus complex a "social and cultural" phenomenon does not alter the decisiveness of parent-child relations for personality development.

I found in Freud much of the explanation for the difficulties that psychologists and psychiatrists have had with saying what they mean by "repression." For Freud's own writings do not anywhere contain an adequate account of the theory of repression to which an investigator might turn in designing his study, or an evaluator in seeking to appraise the results of such studies. Freud's writings are not systematic statements of his theory; they are in the nature of theoretical notebooks by an explorer who was always pushing into new territory, and always changing one or another aspect of his complex set of concepts with every turn of the trail. He not only set out new outposts everywhere along the trail, he often never returned to develop these rudimentary settlements. What is most confusing is the fact that, having changed some crucial aspect of his theory, he seldom went back and revised his other ideas that the change had outdated. In Chapter XI of *Inhibitions, Symptoms and Anxiety*, as we will see in more detail in a later chapter of the present volume, Freud announced just such a fundamental change in the theory of repression, but failed to go back to the preceding ten chapters and correct his own now erroneous statements.

The truth is that Freud, acknowledged genius that he was as an innovator, simply had no interest in or gift for developing a systematic theory. It is doubtful whether he himself could have said, at the end, just what his theory was in a way that would have presented the reader with a clearly developed whole and done justice to its infinite richness and ramifying complexities.

Some psychologists, noting the inconsistency, vagueness, and baffling complexity of Freud's theoretical formulations, have favored translating his theory into a different set of terms altogether. But to do so is usually to distort Freud's meaning, and always to lose the richness of his work. There is nothing for it but to study Freud with the greatest care and put together for ourselves a picture of his theory that will be adequate for scientific evaluation and work. Until this is done, none will be able to say whether a given piece of research is a test of Freud's theory, or whether a new formulation by others is really different or only represents a restatement of Freud.

Psychoanalysts interested in theory have often said that all of Freud's concepts need such intensive study and systematic clarification, but psychologists cannot wait for psychoanalysts to do the job for them. Our discipline stands firmly within the contemporary framework of science; psychoanalysis does not, and without such an orientation on the part of the clarifier, it is doubtful that a statement of Freud's theory can be pro-

6

duced which would be of use to those within science. We must proceed on our own.

The difficulty we face immediately is that Freud's development of the repression theory began in 1893 and did not stop until the 1930's; it is necessary to piece together bit by bit from a great mass of writings, filling twenty-four volumes of the Standard Edition, the web of ideas that, taken together, make up the theory. For the theory must be treated as a whole. The famous 1915 paper on "Repression," or any paper, or any ten, are not enough. To select one feature, such as was done with the extraction of amnesic forgetting, or to take an idea out of historical context, and proceed to test the fragment without attention to the whole invites just the kind of costly waste of resources in research that has characterized studies of psychoanalytic concepts in the past.

The "whole," in the case of the theory of repression, proves to be virtually unextractable from the main theory of psychoanalysis simply because repression is to psychoanalysis as the steel framework is to a modern skyscraper. Or to change the metaphor somewhat, "The theory of repression is the corner-stone on which the whole structure of psychoanalysis rests" (1914a, p. 16). It is indeed less a question of extracting than of portraying the theory in its relation to the rest of psychoanalysis. As Freud himself said, "It is possible to take repression as the center and to bring all the elements of psycho-analytic theory into relation with it" (1925b, p. 30).

Consider the theory of the unconscious, and later of the id. While, strictly speaking, more is at issue in both than what is repressed, both concepts would be quite unimportant except that they refer to repressed material.

The same is true of the dream theory. It not only developed out of Freud's interest in repression, but the main idea of the dreamwork mechanisms, the censor, latent and manifest content, all are elaborations of the repression concept.

The theory of childhood influence rests upon repression. It is basically a theory of the persistence of emotional habits; in Freud's psychology, this persistence is accounted for principally by the notion that repressed ideas are free from normal influences that change habits.

The theory of the ego, id, and superego is founded on repression. Repression creates and maintains the barrier between id and ego; without repression they would be one. The superego is mainly created by the repression of the Oedipus complex.

The Freudian theory of therapy concerns the undoing of repression. The analyst makes repressed ideas and emotions conscious through his interpretations and cure follows if these can be successfully assimilated by the patient.

The sex theory, traditional hallmark of Freudian psychology, and often naively identified as its essence, depends upon repression. Manifest non-sexual motives cannot be identified as "pregenital" or "sexual" without assuming that they are repressively distorted versions of such childhood impulses or of adult sex. The equation "pregenital = sex" can only be successfully argued in terms of repressively transformed impulses.

If the foregoing statements are correct, a study of Freud's repression theory is a study of the most important concept in the most important theory of personality in contemporary psychology and psychiatry. It is a study of the main idea that has been used in the attempt to understand the nation's leading health problem. These are the reasons that not only led me deeper and deeper into Freud, but convinced me I should set down the results of my research in the form of this book, for the picture of repression that emerged bears little relation to the conceptions of it that appear in the literature of psychology, psychiatry, and psychoanalysis.

The first point that became clear was that repression is not a separate concept from defense. The two overlap along virtually their whole extent. The congeries of ideas involved can only be understood as a theory of repression *and* defense.

My long study of Freud's bewildering usage of both terms finally brought a clarifying insight that allowed me to make sense of his whole theory. At first I felt that Freud was impossibly inconsistent. He seemed to equate repression and amnesia in one paper and to speak of conversion and projection and as many as eight similar defenses as "forms of repression" in later ones. "Repression" seemed now to refer to distortions of conscious representation, now to inhibitions of feeling and behavior. It was applied to a great variety of events that occurred in the form of resistance in therapy and also to what had happened in the "primal repressions" of childhood. It covered the responses of neurotics in which impulses were merely disguised and the "destruction in the id" of the Oedipus complex in normal development. Regression and sublimation seemed to be about the only meanings to which Freud never applied the term — and even these came under "repression" when he used the word as a general synonym for "all defenses."

Finally I realized that *none* of these were repression or defense, any more than changes of volume, color, conductivity, or pressure are heat. Just as "heat" refers theoretically to hypothesized atomic vibrations or molecular motion, so "repression" and "defense" refer to the hypothesized interplay of force and counterforce (instincts and anticathexis) in psychic life. Just as heat energy becomes manifest in the volumetric expansion of solids or liquids, in the alteration of their electrical resistivity, in the color changes in metals, or in the psychological sensation of hotness to touch, so the interplay of instinct and anticathexis becomes manifest in a wide variety of effects upon psychological processes. Amnesia was simply the historically first-described manifestation of this interplay of force and counterforce. Resistances, emotional and behavioral inhibitions, and childhood repressions were eventually seen to be new alternative types of manifestation.

This book is the story of these developments in the theory of repression and defense. Part One presents Freud's complex formulations in full. While this can stand alone as an account of Freud's theory, it is meant as a prelude to the eventual objective, which is to formulate the theory in clear and consistent terms at the abstract level, and to relate this theoretical language to an observational language that refers to events directly perceived.

The useful distinction between a theoretical and an observational language has been developed by contemporary philosophers of science. The particular terms are Carnap's: "In discussions of the methodology of science, it is customary and useful to divide the language of science into two parts, the observation language and the theoretical language. The observation language uses terms designating observable properties and relations for the description of observable things or events. The theoretical language, on the other hand, contains terms which may refer to unobservable events, to unobservable features of events, e.g., to microparticles like electrons or atoms, to the electromagnetic field or the gravitational field in physics, to drives and potentials of various kinds in psychology, etc." (6, p. 38.)

The final goal of expressing repression and defense in a theoretical and observational language cannot be reached directly. Such a statement is

9

achieved in Part Two of this book, but it can be comprehensible only after the hard study of Freud that will occupy us in Part One.

The task of this book, then, is to clarify one of the most important concepts of our day. It is not so urgent to study repression "as Freud meant it" just to have a historically correct account of his thinking. It *is* scientifically urgent to achieve conceptual clarification of such an important body of ideas. This book concerns itself only with Freud, a choice and limitation dictated by the obvious desirability of beginning with the originator and most important exponent of the theory and the practical necessity of restricting the scope of the volume. If the task of clarifying repression is to be completed, the thinking of those who have followed Freud must be studied to determine the relationship of subsequent usage to this more comprehensive picture of Freud's theory. The present effort is intended only as "step one."

PART ONE · THE THEORY

✕ Prologue to Part One

IN ORDER to present as complete a statement of Freud's theory of repression as possible — sufficiently full so that the scholar or research worker need not restudy all of Freud's works for himself — Part One relies heavily on Freud's own words. One or more quotations are given for every aspect of the theory discussed. Without such direct evidence Freudian scholars might well dispute some of the points made, since the argument that develops is not the one that is familiar either to psychologists or to psychoanalysts.

The frequent quotations make the reading difficult, for besides the pertinent evidence they contribute to the point at issue here, they often necessarily include other material that is, in the context, irrelevant. To meet the needs of the reader whose purposes do not require that he see the evidence for himself, and to provide a concise restatement that may be used by all readers for review, each chapter is followed by a summary. If read alone these summaries give a full account of Freud's theory of repression; but for the supporting evidence of Freud's own words one must turn to the earlier sections of each chapter.

The materials in Part One are put in historical perspective. I want to emphasize the importance of this. Determining what Freud's theory was at different points in the development of psychoanalysis is no mere scholastic exercise; too often psychologists have spent valuable time refuting ideas or testing theories that had been tried and then given up by Freud. Heinz Hartmann has pointed to this problem: ". . . without such historical reference it happens over and over again that analytical hypotheses are dealt with on one level, so to say, which belong to different phases of theory formation, and some of which have actually been discarded and

13

replaced by others" (12, p. 5). I hope that what follows (although at times it may seem that I am belaboring the obvious) will help forestall costly mistakes of this kind.

The reader will find that the otherwise bewildering material of Part One will fit readily into an easily understood whole if he keeps in mind the simplifying generalization that these chapters describe alternative manifestations of repression and defense. Repression and defense should be thought of as referring, theoretically, to unseen and unseeable events — to an imaginatively represented interplay of instinctual forces and anti-forces within the person. This interplay results in varied behavioral effects which *are* observable — resistances, symptoms, dreams, distortions of conscious representation, amnesia, inhibitions, and certain childhood fears. The chapters of Part One describe these varied manifestations of the hypothesized interaction between force and counterforce as they appeared in Freud's writings.

I

✕. Repression *and* Defense

T H E most difficult and persistent problem in the theory of repression is the relation between repression and defense.

Freudian scholars agree that the earliest meaning for "repression" was amnesic forgetting as seen in hysterical cases in which painful events of the patient's past could not be recalled. This remained as one constant meaning of the term throughout the years. They agree, too, that Freud also introduced the term "defense" almost at the start and used the two words interchangeably for a time, both with this limited meaning and in a more general sense. Gradually the term "defense" dropped out of Freud's writings except for an occasional use, and for several decades "repression" was Freud's main term. In 1926 he proposed readopting "defense" to designate all forms of ego-protection against inner impulses which the person treats as dangerous. "Repression," he indicated, would be reserved for its original and specific meaning of amnesic forgetting.

So far as the psychoanalytic literature is concerned, that is the story of repression and defense and their relationship to one another — a simple case of overlapping usage of terms which was settled once and for all in 1926 when the matter came to Freud's attention while he was writing *Inhibitions, Symptoms and Anxiety.*

The material assembled in the present chapter challenges this. I propose to show that the limited meaning of "repression," while constant over the years, was a minor referent of the term; that "repression" soon came to refer to a general theory of broad scope that was so fundamental to psychoanalytic theory as a whole that Freud rightly called it the cornerstone of his conception of psychology; and that this general theory became and *continued throughout to be* the principal meaning of "repression."

15

Freud, it will be my intent to prove, was never able to maintain the distinction he proposed in 1926, in which "repression" was subordinated to "defense" — not even within the very volume in which he announced it. This might be dismissed as mere inconsistency, or attributed to the sheer weight of twenty years of habitual usage of "repression" as the main term for the general theory; but I believe rather that this failure lay in the nature of the repression concept itself — that its fundamental meaning made it impossible to separate "repression" and "defense," that in their most important sense the terms are so inextricably bound to one set of ideas that a separation is not possible within the framework of Freud's theory. Hence what we have is, in fact, not a theory of repression and a more general theory of defense, but one firmly fused theory of repression *and* defense.

REPRESSION AS AMNESIA

The first appearance of the term "repressed" occurred in the famous "Preliminary Communication" paper by Breuer and Freud in 1893, later republished as Chapter I of *Studies on Hysteria*: "In the first group are those cases in which the patients have not reacted to a psychical trauma because the nature of the trauma excluded a reaction, as in the case of the apparently irreparable loss of a loved person or because social circumstances made a reaction impossible or because it was a question of things which the patient wished to forget, and therefore intentionally repressed from his conscious thought and inhibited and suppressed" (1895, p. 10).

There is general agreement that in this initial use "repression" meant unconsciously motivated forgetting, which was described with particular clarity in the following passage: "These patients whom I analysed had enjoyed good mental health up to the time at which an intolerable idea presented itself within the content of their ideational life; that is to say, until their ego was confronted by an experience, an idea, a feeling, arousing an affect so painful that the person resolved to forget it, since he had no confidence in his power to resolve the incompatibility between the unbearable idea and his ego by the processes of thought" (1894, pp. 61–62).

The use of such phrases as "intentionally repressed" and "resolved to forget" in his early writings has led some to question whether Freud first

16

viewed hysterical amnesia as being unconsciously motivated. Brenner (4, p. 23) feels that Freud at first considered repression to be a conscious, voluntary act. But the editors of the Standard Edition of Freud's work remarked that Freud's use of "intentionally" in the first quotation above ". . . merely indicates the existence of a motive and carries no implication of *conscious* intention" (1895, p. 10). At any rate, the idea that the motivated forgetting was unconscious did become a clear principle with Freud within a few years (by 1896).

The use of "repression" to refer specifically to hysterical amnesia, or unconsciously motivated forgetting, continued unchanged throughout the whole period of Freud's writings. In 1926 he reaffirmed this usage in *Inhibitions, Symptoms and Anxiety*: "Our first observations of repression and of the formation of symptoms were made in connection with hysteria. We found that the perceptual content of exciting experiences and the ideational content of pathogenic structures of thought were forgotten and debarred from being reproduced in memory, and we therefore concluded that the keeping away from consciousness was a main characteristic of hysterical repression." (1926a, p. 163.)

If matters had stopped here, there would be no need for research into what the term "repression" meant to Freud, but its meaning grew more complex with every development in psychoanalytic theory. The only uncontroversial point is that the meaning of "repression" as hysterical amnesia came first and was never abandoned.

"DEFENSE" AS A SYNONYM FOR "REPRESSION"

There was an almost immediate complication when Freud introduced the term "defense" and used it as a synonym for "repression." Thus he designated cases showing hysterical amnesia as cases of "defence hysteria" (1894, p. 61). These lines taken from the Preface to the first edition of *Studies on Hysteria* show how Breuer and Freud used the two words as synonyms: "Thus it comes about that we are only able to produce very incomplete evidence in favor of our view that sexuality seems to play a principal part in the pathogenesis of hysteria as a source of psychical traumas and as a motive for 'defence'— that is, for repressing ideas from consciousness" (1895, p. xxix).

Similarly: ". . . symptoms arise through the psychical mechanism of (unconscious) defence, that is, through an attempt to repress an intolerable idea. . . . In . . . *Studien über Hysterie* I have been able by quoting clinical observations to elucidate and illustrate what is meant by the psychical process of 'defence' or 'repression'." (1896, p. 155.)

These quotations indicate that, at this point, "repression" and "defense" were synonyms.

OTHER DEFENSES AS FORMS OF REPRESSION

A second complication in the meaning of "repression" in relation to "defense" also arose in Freud's very first papers on psychoanalysis. Having conceived hysterical amnesia as a manifestation of "defense," Freud quickly applied his new-found terminology to other forms of mental illness, including certain phobias, obsessional neuroses, and some paranoias, which he called "defence neuro-psychoses" in his 1894 and 1896 papers. In these same papers he described further mental mechanisms beyond hysterical amnesia, including conversion, projection, and substitution — and, in introducing these new terms, he specifically called each one a "form of repression."

Conversion. "In hysteria the unbearable idea is rendered innocuous by the quantity of excitation attached to it being transmuted into some bodily form of expression, a process for which I should like to propose the name of *conversion*" (1894, p. 63). Again: ". . . in hysteria the repression is effectively established by means of *conversion* into bodily innervation" (1896, p. 169).

Projection. "In paranoia the reproach is repressed in a manner which may be described as *projection*; by the defence-symptom of *distrust directed against others* being erected; in this way recognition of the reproach is withheld, and, as if in return, protection is lost against the self-reproaches which appear in the delusions" (1896, p. 180).

Substitution (Displacement, Transposition). ". . . the repression is effectively established . . . in the obsessional neurosis by means of *substitution* (displacement along certain associated channels)" (1896, p. 169).

Isolation. In 1909, in his analysis of the "rat-man" case, Freud similarly designated isolation as a mechanism of repression: "In hysteria it is the rule that the precipitating causes of the illness are overtaken by an amnesia. . . . In this amnesia we see the evidence of the repression which has taken place. The case is different in obsessional neuroses. The infantile preconditions of the neurosis may be overtaken by amnesia, though

18

this is often an incomplete one; but the immediate occasions of the illness are, on the contrary, retained in the memory. Repression makes use of another, and in reality simpler, mechanism. The trauma, instead of being forgotten, is deprived of its affective cathexis; so that what remains in consciousness is nothing but its ideational content, which is perfectly colourless and is judged to be unimportant." (1909, pp. 195–96.)

Of course, calling conversion, projection, substitution, and isolation forms of repression was consistent with the use of "repression" as a synonym for "defense," and this consistency is one kind of evidence that "repression" and "defense" were, in this period, alternative terms. At the same time, Freud in these papers continued to use "repression" in the more specific meaning of hysterical amnesia, but did not discuss this double usage.

DROPPING OF "DEFENSE" FROM FREUD'S USAGE

After the early years Freud used the term "defense" infrequently until the 1926 *Inhibitions, Symptoms and Anxiety*. In 1906 he himself pointed this out: "As a consequence, accidental influences receded still further into the background as compared with 'repression' (as I now began to say instead of 'defence') . . . Apart from this, accidental influences have been replaced by constitutional factors and 'defence' in the purely psychological sense has been replaced by organic 'sexual repression'." (1906, pp. 276, 278.)

Freud did not explain why he dropped "defense" from his terminology for some twenty years, just as earlier he had said nothing about the use of "repression" and "defense" as synonyms. The least that can be inferred is that he must have felt two terms were unnecessary to cover a single meaning. The fact that he could get along for the several decades of his most productive writing without "defense" is clear evidence that he had developed a general theory of repression of which amnesic forgetting was only a minor aspect.

"REPRESSION" IN 1915

Freud's 1915 article on "Repression" is considered to be his definitive statement of the concept. His formal definition of the term was ". . . that *the essence of repression lies simply in turning something away, and keeping it at a distance, from the conscious*" (1915b, p. 147).

It is to be noted that this definition does not restrict repression to amnesia. *Any* means of keeping material "at a distance from the conscious" can be considered repression. That such generality was intentional on Freud's part is shown by the fact that later in the article he asked whether there are not different mechanisms of repression: "We must now try to obtain some insight into the *mechanism* of the process of repression. In particular we want to know whether there is a single mechanism only, or more than one, and whether each of the psychoneuroses is distinguished by a mechanism of repression peculiar to it." (1915b, pp. 153–54.)

Freud went on to examine repression in phobias, conversion hysteria, and obsessional neuroses and his discussion makes it wholly clear that, in this crucial article, the term "repression" is being used in the broad sense of defense. Since Freud was examining the problem of the relation of symptoms and substitute formations (displacements), the material does not lend itself as easily as one would wish to quotations bearing precisely on the relation of repression and defense, but I have extracted some relevant statements from the complicating discussion of symptoms and substitute formations:

"From the field of *anxiety hysteria* I will choose a well-analysed example of an animal phobia. The instinctual impulse subjected to repression here is a libidinal attitude towards the father, coupled with fear of him. After repression, this impulse vanishes out of consciousness. . . . A repression such as occurs in an animal phobia must be described as radically unsuccessful . . . We are obliged to take quite another view of the process of repression when we consider the picture of a true *conversion hysteria.* . . . In conversion hysteria the process of repression is completed with the formation of the symptom. . . . A totally different picture of repression is shown . . . in *obsessional neurosis.* . . . From this we learn something, too, about the mechanism of repression. In this instance, as in all others, repression has brought about a withdrawal of libido; but here it has made use of *reaction-formation* for this purpose, by intensifying an opposite." (1915b, pp. 155–57 with extensive omissions.)

In these parts of the 1915 paper on "Repression," then, Freud clearly used the term to refer to a general concept that included other defenses as particular forms of repression, as he had done in the 1896 period.

But the situation is not as clear-cut as this suggests. Freud was inconsistent within the paper itself. Consider this passage: ". . . repression is not a defensive mechanism which is present from the very beginning, and

. . . it cannot arise until a sharp cleavage has occurred between conscious and unconscious mental activity . . . *the essence of repression lies simply in turning something away, and keeping it at a distance, from the conscious.* This view of repression would be made more complete by assuming that, before the mental organization reaches this stage, the task of fending off instinctual impulses is dealt with by the other vicissitudes which instincts may undergo — e.g. reversal into the opposite or turning round upon the subject's own self." (1915b, p. 147.)

Here the term "defensive mechanism" definitely suggests that repression is *one* mechanism among a larger number, and certainly that, early in life, reversal and turning round on the self are distinctive defense mechanisms ("vicissitudes") that differ from repression. While Freud does not explicitly speak of a general conception of defense in the paper, clearly this idea is present.

On the basis of this passage, and his study of Freud's other 1915 papers, Charles Brenner concluded: "It is clear, therefore, that Freud in 1915 no longer considered 'defense' and 'repression' to be synonymous" (4, p. 36). But Brenner's conclusion simply does not respect the genuine inconsistency in the article. He is partly correct, but his position does not make sense of the main sections of the article, particularly the discussion, quoted earlier, of the different forms of repression in the three neuroses. The editor of the translation of the paper in the Standard Edition agrees that "It is, indeed, in this wider sense that the term ["repression"] is used in the present paper" (Volume XIV, p. 144).

"REPRESSION" AND "DEFENSE" IN 1926

Whatever their interpretation of Freud's usage of "repression" and "defense" in the 1915 period, all authorities are agreed that Freud finally settled the problem for good in his 1926 *Inhibitions, Symptoms and Anxiety*:

"In the course of discussing the problem of anxiety I have revived a concept or, to put it more modestly, a term, of which I made exclusive use thirty years ago when I first began to study the subject but which I later abandoned. I refer to the term 'defensive process'. I afterwards replaced it by the word 'repression', but the relation between the two remained uncertain. It will be an undoubted advantage, I think, to revert to the old concept of 'defence', provided we employ it explicitly as a general designation for all the techniques which the ego makes use of in conflicts which may lead to a neurosis, while we retain the word 'repression' for the special method of defence which the line of approach taken by our investigations made us better acquainted with in the first instance.

"Even a purely terminological innovation ought to justify its adoption; it ought to reflect some new point of view or some extension of knowledge. The revival of the concept of defence and the restriction of that of repression takes into account a fact which has long since been known but which has received added importance owing to some new discoveries. Our first observations of repression and of the formation of symptoms were made in connection with hysteria. We found that the perceptual content of exciting experiences and the ideational content of pathogenic structures of thought were forgotten and debarred from being reproduced in memory, and we therefore concluded that the keeping away from consciousness was a main characteristic of hysterical repression. Later on, when we came to study the obsessional neuroses, we found that in that illness pathogenic occurrences are not forgotten. They remain conscious but they are 'isolated' in some way that we cannot as yet grasp, so that much the same result is obtained as in hysterical amnesia. Nevertheless the difference is great enough to justify the belief that the process by which instinctual demands are set aside in obsessional neurosis cannot be the same as in hysteria. Further investigations have shown that in obsessional neurosis a regression of the instinctual impulses to an earlier libidinal stage is brought about through the opposition of the ego, and that this regression, although it does not make repression unnecessary, clearly works in the same sense as repression. We have seen, too, that in obsessional neurosis anticathexis, which is also presumably present in hysteria, plays a specially large part in protecting the ego by effecting a reactive alteration in it. Our attention has, moreover, been drawn to a process of 'isolation' (whose technique cannot as yet be elucidated), which finds direct symptomatic manifestation, and to a procedure, that may be called magical, of 'undoing' what has been done — a procedure about whose defensive purpose there can be no doubt, but which has no longer any resemblance to the process of 'repression'. These observations provide good enough grounds for re-introducing the old concept of *defence*, which can cover all these processes that have the same purpose — namely, the protection of the ego against instinctual demands — and for subsuming repression under it as a special case." (1926a, pp. 163–64.)

Freud's decision to adopt a consistent usage for "repression" — mean-

22

ing amnesic forgetting (as in hysteria) — and "defense" — the over-all term, including repression as one of ten or so defenses — would have introduced a much-needed clarification. But to make it meaningful would have required rewriting many of his previous discussions, particularly his paper of 1915 that defined "repression" in terms of keeping material at a distance from consciousness, a function that is performed quite as well by reaction-formation or projection as by amnesia.

Not only did he neglect to do this rewriting, he did not even carry out his new resolution in the very same book in which it was proposed, where we find him describing reaction-formation, reversal, undoing, and isolation as *forms of repression*, exactly as he had done with conversion, projection, and substitution in 1896, and isolation in 1909 :

Reaction-Formation. "Conflicts of this kind due to ambivalence are very frequent and they can have another typical outcome, in which one of the two conflicting feelings (usually that of affection) becomes enormously intensified and the other vanishes. The exaggerated degree and compulsive character of the affection alone betray the fact that it is not the only one present but is continually on the alert to keep the opposite feeling under suppression, and enable us to postulate the operation of a process which we call repression by means of *reaction-formation* (in the ego)." (1926a, p. 102.)

Reversal. "The case of the 'Wolf Man' and the somewhat less complicated one of 'Little Hans' raise a number of further considerations. But we have already made two unexpected discoveries. There can be no doubt that the instinctual impulse which was repressed in both phobias was a hostile one against the father. One might say that that impulse had been repressed by the process of being transformed into its opposite. Instead of aggressiveness on the part of the subject towards his father, there appeared aggressiveness (in the shape of revenge) on the part of his father towards the subject." (1926a, p. 106.)

Undoing. "The two techniques I refer to are *undoing what has been done* and *isolating*. The first of these has a wide range of application and goes back very far. It is, as it were, negative magic, and endeavours, by means of motor symbolism, to 'blow away' not merely the *consequences* of some event (or experience or impression) but the event itself. . . . This endeavour to undo shades off into normal behaviour in the case in which a person decides to regard an event as not having happened. But whereas he will take no direct steps against the event, and will simply

23

pay no further attention to it or its consequences, the neurotic person will try to make the past itself non-existent. He will try to repress it by motor means. The same purpose may perhaps account for the obsession for *repeating* which is so frequently met with in this neurosis and the carrying out of which serves a number of contradictory intentions at once. When anything has not happened in the desired way it is undone by being repeated in a different way; and thereupon all the motives that exist for lingering over such repetitions come into play as well. As the neurosis proceeds, we often find that the endeavour to undo a traumatic experience is a motive of first-rate importance in the formation of symptoms. We thus unexpectedly discover a new, motor technique of defence, or (as we may say in this case with less inaccuracy) of repression." (1926a, pp. 119, 120.)

Isolation. In speaking of the two clinically related defenses of isolation and undoing Freud refers to them as "variations of repression" (1926a, p. 119). He goes on to say: "The second of these techniques which we are setting out to describe for the first time, that of isolation, is peculiar to obsessional neurosis. It, too, takes place in the motor sphere. When something unpleasant has happened to the subject or when he himself has done something which has a significance for his neurosis, he interpolates an interval during which nothing further must happen — during which he must perceive nothing and do nothing. This behaviour, which seems strange at first sight, is soon seen to have a relation to repression. We know that in hysteria it is possible to cause a traumatic experience to be overtaken by amnesia. In obsessional neurosis this can often not be achieved: the experience is not forgotten, but, instead, it is deprived of its affect, and its associative connections are suppressed or interrupted so that it remains as though isolated and is not reproduced in the ordinary processes of thought. The effect of this isolation is the same as the effect of repression with amnesia. This technique, then, is reproduced in the isolations of obsessional neurosis; and it is at the same time given motor reinforcement for magical purposes." (1926a, p. 120.)

Not only does Freud specifically call each of these defenses a "form of repression," in the same book he continues to use "repression" and "defense" as general synonyms for one another: ". . . is it absolutely certain that fear of castration is the only motive force behind repression (or defence) . . . When, in analysis, we have given the ego assistance which is able to put it in a position to lift its repressions, it recovers its

24

power over the repressed id . . . we find that even after the ego has decided to relinquish its resistances it still has difficulty in undoing the repressions . . ." (1926a, pp. 123, 154, 159.)

If Freud had been using "repression" to mean hysterical amnesia only, in each of these quotations he would have had to write "defense" at the points where, in fact, he wrote "repression." In one case he recognized his continuing double usage by inserting "defense" in parentheses after having written "repression."

It is true that Freud's resolution to separate these terms is contained in a final chapter of *Inhibitions, Symptoms and Anxiety* that is labeled "Addenda," while the inconsistencies pointed out above are in the main text; and it is likely that the text had been written before the thoughts contained in the "Addenda" were formulated by Freud. But it seems curious that he did not go back and clarify his terminology in the early chapters. A reasonable explanation is that the problem was a deeper one than merely deciding upon a simple terminological convention.

"REPRESSION" AND "DEFENSE" AFTER 1926

What about after 1926? Again, there is the same inconsistency of usage. Sometimes Freud clearly treated repression as simply one defense among many, as in 1937: ". . . the ego makes use of various methods of fulfilling its task, *i.e.*, to put it in general terms, of avoiding danger, anxiety and unpleasure. We call these devices *defensive mechanisms* . . .

"One of these mechanisms, that of repression, provided the starting-point for the study of neurotic processes in general. There was never any doubt that repression was not the only method which the ego could employ for its purposes. Nevertheless, repression is something quite peculiar, more sharply differentiated from the other mechanisms than these are from one another. I should like to make its relation to these other mechanisms clear by an analogy, but I know that analogies never carry us very far in such matters.

"Let us imagine what might have happened to a book at the time when books were not printed in editions but written out separately by hand. We will imagine that such a book contained statements which at a later time were regarded as undesirable — as, for instance, according to Robert Eisler (1929), the writings of Flavius Josephus must have contained passages about Jesus Christ which were offensive to later Christendom. At the present day the only defensive mechanism to which the official

25

censorship would resort would be the confiscation and destruction of every copy of the whole edition. At that time other methods were employed to render the book innocuous. Either the offensive passages were heavily scored through, so that they were illegible, in which case they could not be transcribed and the next copyist of the book produced a text to which no exception could be taken but which had gaps in certain places, probably making the passages in question unintelligible. Or, not satisfied with this, the authorities tried to conceal any indication that the text had been mutilated. They therefore proceeded to tamper with the text. Single words here and there were left out or replaced by others and whole new sentences were interpolated; at best, the passage was completely erased and replaced by another in exactly the opposite sense. When the book was next transcribed the text aroused no suspicion, but had, in fact, been falsified. It no longer contained the author's statement and very probably the correction was not in the interests of truth.

"Without pressing the analogy too closely we may say that repression is to the other methods of defence what the omission of words or passages is to the corruption of a text, and in the various forms of this falsification we can discover parallels to the manifold ways in which the ego may be modified." (1937, pp. 338–39.)

In this passage, repression is set off as one defense among others and distinctive in its mode of operation, since it creates mental blanks in consciousness — something is absent that should be present — while other defenses distort what is in consciousness. But in the same article "repression" is also used in its broad sense to mean all defenses: "All repressions take place in early childhood; they are primitive defensive measures adopted by the immature, feeble ego . . . Thus the real achievement of analytic therapy would be the subsequent correction of the original process of repression, with the result that the supremacy of the quantitative factor is brought to an end." (1937, pp. 328, 329.)

These two sentences would hardly be meaningful if one substituted "amnesia" at each point where Freud uses "repression." Another 1937 paper shows the same general usage, which Freud himself acknowledges by his parenthetical comment: "It is familiar ground that the work of analysis aims at inducing the patient to give up the repressions (using the word in the widest sense) belonging to his early life and to replace them by reactions of a sort that would correspond better to a psychically mature condition" (1937, pp. 358–59).

26

This multiple usage continued through his final *Outline of Psychoanalysis* in which "defense" and "repressions" are quite explicitly equated: "Driven by the combined power of these two influences, of the immediate real danger and of the remembered phylogenetic one, the child embarks upon his attempts at defense (repressions), which are effective for the moment but nevertheless turn out to be inadequate when the later reanimation of sexual life brings a reinforcement to the repudiated instinctual demands" (1940, pp. 112–13).

THE INSEPARABILITY OF REPRESSION AND MOST FORMS OF DEFENSE

If we are not to interpret four decades of interchangeable usage of "repression" and "defense" as a case of remarkable inconsistency, why was this problem so persistent? Particularly, why could not Freud straighten out his terms after his resolution to do so in *Inhibitions, Symptoms and Anxiety*? My own answer is that the two concepts as Freud had developed them were inseparable because both were inextricably linked to consciousness in a way that did not allow separation through a simple agreement on terminology.

Consider various defenses and their relationship to consciousness. In amnesia the dangerous impulse is dealt with by forgetting the events associated with it. The effect is that the person is not conscious of certain past happenings, and his unawareness prevents him from becoming anxious. Consciousness is tampered with as the means of controlling anxiety.

In reaction-formation the person is consciously preoccupied with thoughts that are opposite to the dangerous impulses. The effect is to distort consciousness as a means of controlling anxiety.

In projection the impulse may be in the person's awareness, but he attributes its ownership to another person. This distortion of consciousness also protects the person from anxiety.

In isolation the dangerous material itself is in consciousness but its relationship to other mental content is not seen by the person. As long as the dangerous ideas are not related to other ideas and emotions with which they would normally go, their implications are not dangerous. The meaning of an idea depends upon its being related to the larger context of the person's thought and feelings. By preventing such a relating, isolation prevents anxiety through this particular distortion of consciousness.

27

In displacement, or substitution, consciousness is once more distorted and anxiety partly controlled by falsely representing the object of the dangerous impulse to be something other than the real object, as when Little Hans feared horses rather than his father.

In conversion the person's psychological problem is represented in his consciousness as a physical disability, and this distortion keeps the person from being overanxious.

In reversal, consciousness is distorted by representing one impulse by its opposite, as when love is represented as hatred.

In each case some sort of tampering with consciousness is the means by which anxiety is lessened. If one were to speak of all these mechanisms as defenses, one would have to define "defense" as the attempt to control anxiety by a distortion of consciousness. Each defense achieves this distortion in a particular way. It is true that amnesic forgetting, as Freud said, achieves an effect on consciousness by *omitting* something which would ordinarily be present, while the others *misrepresent* some aspect of the person's psychological processes. This may be a definable difference, but the essential fact is that in these seven defense mechanisms there is an alteration of conscious representation as a means of controlling anxiety.

Now consider Freud's basic definition of "repression" given in his main article on the concept. Repression, too, centers around the control of consciousness: ". . . *the essence of repression lies simply in turning something away, and keeping it at a distance, from the conscious*" (1915b, p. 147). This definition of "repression" agrees perfectly with the conclusion as to the essential feature of each of a number of defenses. It is hardly surprising that difficulties arose when Freud tried to separate repression and defense.

In point of fact, as I have said, there is no separate concept of repression and one of defense. During the whole period of his writings Freud was using one general idea, the concept of inner psychic forces interacting and producing effects on consciousness and behaviour. Amnesia was simply the first of these effects that Freud studied. As he found others, Freud called them "new forms of repression." If one rephrases this to say that he was describing new manifestations of the same processes that he first described in his conception of hysterical amnesia, a clarifying simplification is introduced into Freud's otherwise bewildering terminological usages. As the foregoing discussion has demonstrated, Freud sometimes referred to *all* these manifestations as defense, and sometimes as repression. In addition he used "repression" in the more specific sense of amnesia.

6/367

SUMMARY

This chapter explores the various meanings of "repression" and "defense" at the points where the two overlap.

"Repression" was first used by Freud in the early studies of hysteria to refer to unconsciously motivated forgetting. This specific meaning of the word continued unchanged throughout all of Freud's writings.

As soon as Freud turned from the study of hysteria to other neuroses, he began distinguishing other defenses such as conversion, projection, displacement, and isolation. He referred to these specifically as "forms of repression"; at the same time, he used "defense" as a synonym to refer to the same mechanisms.

Within a few years, "defense" was dropped from Freud's usage, and "repression" became virtually his only term to refer to the whole problem of defense and the various defense mechanisms. He did, on rare occasions, use "defense," and several times used "vicissitudes" as a synonym for "defense."

Freud's defining paper of 1915 on "Repression" showed clearly that he was not using the term to refer only to amnesic forgetting, but also to a general conception of ego-protection through the manipulation and control of consciousness. He distinguished repression in this consciousness-altering sense from other defenses such as reversal and turning round on the self, which, at least in his 1915 interpretation, did not have the alteration of consciousness as their principal mode of action, and went on to indicate that, in this general meaning of "repression" as used in the paper, displacement, conversion, and reaction-formation were forms of repression.

In a final chapter (entitled "Addenda") of his 1926 *Inhibitions, Symptoms and Anxiety*, Freud suggested a resolution of the problem of his varied usages of "repression" by proposing that he revive the old term "defense" to refer to all forms of ego-protection against dangerous inner impulses, and that "repression" be used only in its original and specific meaning of unconsciously motivated forgetting (as in hysterical amnesia).

Curiously, Freud did not follow his own resolution in the very book in which it was proposed, since throughout the volume he used "repression" to refer to reaction-formation, reversal, and undoing, and indeed used "repression" as a synonym for "defense" in its general meaning. Furthermore, this same multiple usage continued in publications up to his last, along with usages that seemed to conform to the 1926 resolution.

In my judgment, this was not simply a case of inconsistency, but rather resulted from a basic problem stemming apparently from the fact that Freud developed his ideas about repression and defense at an early point when his psychology was particularly concerned with consciousness and unconsciousness. This focus on consciousness led to an interest in the various ways in which conscious representation was altered or distorted in neuroses, ways which he alternately referred to as "forms of repression" and "defenses." Both terms were oriented to ego-protection by means of alterations of consciousness as their principle reference. Probably it was this completely overlapping meaning that led Freud to drop "defense" for several decades.

In conclusion: repression and defense were one concept; there never was, in Freud's writings, except for the briefest periods, a concept of repression that was separate from the concept of defense.

II

Repressive and "Nonrepressive" Defenses

THE preceding chapter explored the varying usages of "repression" and "defense" and concluded that, at their most general level, they had the same meaning. As was suggested, a great clarification of Freud's theory becomes possible if we grasp the fact that the concept of repression and defense had as its main theoretical referent the idea of unobservable inner psychic forces interacting and producing a variety of observable effects. Chapter I mentioned some of these effects. The rest of Part One will attempt to show the whole range of effects on psychological processes resulting from interaction of force and counterforce. In doing this it is useful to distinguish among several general types of these effects, such as effects seen as resistance in therapy, effects on emotional inhibition, and effects on childhood responses to unbearable tension states, with more particular varieties grouped within these broader classes.

REPRESSIVE DEFENSES

We shall begin in the present short chapter with one of these general groupings implicit although not specifically named by Freud in the writings reviewed in Chapter I. Since he used both "repression" and "defense" in referring to the concept underlying this group of effects, it is appropriate to call them "repressive defenses." They may be defined as those mechanisms of ego-protection that rely upon alterations of the conscious representation of dangerous-impulse-associated mental content as their principal means of controlling anxiety. Repressive defenses include amnesia, conversion, reaction-formation, projection, displacement (substitution), isolation, undoing, and denial.

Repressive defenses were the first to be distinguished by Freud, and it seems probable that their common orientation around alterations of conscious representation as a means of controlling anxiety reflects the fact that psychoanalysis historically began with the study of consciousness and unconsciousness.

There is some suggestive evidence in his 1915 paper on "Instincts and Their Vicissitudes" that Freud himself moved in the direction of recognizing a classification that set off repressive defenses from other defenses. There Freud commented: "Observation shows us that an instinct may undergo the following vicissitudes: —

> Reversal into its opposite.
> Turning round upon the subject's own self.
> Repression.
> Sublimation.

Since I do not intend to treat of sublimation here and since repression requires a special chapter to itself, it only remains for us to describe and discuss the two first points. Bearing in mind that there are motive forces which work against an instinct's being carried through in an unmodified form we may also regard these vicissitudes as modes of *defence* against the instincts." (1915a, pp. 126–127.)

There are at least two points of interest about this 1915 classification of defenses. One is that repression is separated off from the other three as being based upon some property not shared with the rest. Secondly, most of the defenses that are herein called repressive defenses are not listed, even though they had regularly been a part of Freud's writings on repression and defense in the years preceding this paper. There is, then, the definite possibility that the "repression" Freud lists is intended to cover such other defenses, rather than only amnesic forgetting, especially since this particular article was one of a theoretical series of which the "Repression" paper was the next written. It will be recalled that it was in this latter paper that Freud defined repression as ". . . *turning something away, and keeping it at a distance, from the conscious"* (1915b, p. 147). As I pointed out earlier, this definition is far broader than amnesia, and clearly covers what I have called repressive defenses.

The possibility that "repression" in this 1915 "Vicissitudes" classification meant, in fact, repressive defenses is further heightened by Freud's reasons, given in the immediately following "Repression" paper, for listing reversal and turning round upon the self as defenses to be distinguished

32

from repression. In that paper Freud said: ". . . repression is not a defensive mechanism which is present from the very beginning, and . . . it cannot arise until a sharp cleavage has occurred between conscious and unconscious mental activity. . . . before the mental organization reaches this stage, the task of fending off instinctual impulses is dealt with by the other vicissitudes which instincts may undergo — e.g. reversal into the opposite or turning round upon the subject's own self." (1915b, p. 147.)

In other words, reversal and turning round upon the self, Freud is saying, do not have the alteration of consciousness as their main means of achieving ego-protection. These two defenses must result in some effect upon consciousness, since in reversal an opposite impulse replaces the dangerous one and in turning round on the self the direction of the impulse is altered from being toward others to being toward self; but their effects on consciousness, Freud believed in 1915, cannot be any primary matter, since consciousness and unconsciousness have not yet appeared as a definite dichotomy in mental life.

It is also to be noticed that Freud lists sublimation as a separate defense in the vicissitudes classification. As we will see in a later chapter, sublimation is based primarily upon the idea of one drive actually replacing another, rather than upon conscious misrepresentation of the drive state. Hence, Freud's listing it separately would help confirm the hypothesis that "repression" meant repressive defenses in the 1915 classification.

Interpreted in this light the 1915 classification would read:

1. Reversal
2. Turning round upon the self
3. Sublimation
4. Repressive defenses

a. Amnesia	e. Reaction-formation
b. Conversion	f. Isolation
c. Displacement	g. Undoing
d. Projection	h. Denial

This classification helps to make the 1915 "Repression" paper intelligible. As it stands, it is not a paper on amnesic repression; not only is "repression" defined in broad terms as the control of conscious representations of dangerous impulse material, but, at the end of the paper, displacement, conversion, and reaction-formation are all called mechanisms of repression. At the same time it is not a paper on defense in its broadest sense of all ego-protective mechanisms, since Freud explicitly differentiates between repression as used in the paper and reversal and turning round on the self, both of which he calls "vicissitudes," a term he used as a synonym for "defense" in the 1915 period. The whole paper becomes meaningful if it is seen as a discussion of repressive defense, a concept which was implicit in Freud's thinking and for which he did not have a separate name.

"NONREPRESSIVE" DEFENSES

Repressive defenses stand in contrast to defenses that do not use alterations of consciousness as their main means of ego-protection. Although these can logically be called "nonrepressive defenses," the term does not recommend itself despite its formal correctness. Unlike the group of repressive defenses, "nonrepressive defenses" are not united by any common principle other than the negative one that they are *not* repressive defenses. Furthermore, the term itself lacks the right connotations. Nevertheless, since some such term is needed it will be used where it will contribute to the clarity of the discussion.

In this section we shall consider regression as an example of such a "nonrepressive" defense.

Following the early period in which he focused on the conscious and unconcious, Freud turned particularly to the study of personality from childhood to maturity, an investigation begun in *Three Essays on the Theory of Sexuality* in 1905. As a part of this new interest, Freud conceived several further defenses that were particularly oriented to development through the life span rather than to the conscious and unconscious. Regression and sublimation were two of these, joined, in later years, by such concepts as "desexualization," "absorption," and "destruction in the id." Of these various "developmental defenses," regression offers the most instructive contrast to repressive defenses.

Freud distinguished two types of regression: "a return to the first objects invested with libido, which we know to be incestuous in character, and a return of the whole sexual organization to earlier stages" (1916–17, p. 299). In the first case a non-incestuous sex interest is given up because it is too fraught with frustrations and the person returns to an earlier form of sex interest, one he had had as a child: the Oedipal interest in a parent. In the second, the frustrations of attempting to live on a mature genital level lead the person to return to an even earlier pregenital sex interest, and he substitutes an oral or anal sex interest for the abandoned genital one.

It is the second type of regression that is in particularly sharp contrast to repressive defenses, because it involves the replacement of one drive by another. This replacement is seen in obsessional neuroses, where ". . . regression of the libido to the antecedent stage of the sadistic-anal organization is the most conspicuous factor and determines the form taken by the symptoms. The impulse to love must then mask itself under the sadistic impulse. The obsessive thought, 'I should like to murder you', means . . . nothing else but 'I should like to enjoy love of you'." (1916–17, p. 301.)

The substitution of drives in regression involves impulses that are conceived by Freud to have a developmental relationship to one another. The anal-sadistic drives are held to precede the genital in the normal sequence, and in regression they replace the abandoned genital drive. This principle is stated both in the quotation directly above and also in the one on page 36 below, and is amplified in detail in Freud's chapter on "Aspects of Development and Regression" in *A General Introduction to Psychoanalysis*.

This principle of substitution differs from that found in repressive defenses such as reaction-formation and conversion, where the capacity of the substitute impulse to *disguise* the underlying repressed one is the chief consideration. In obsessional neuroses the substitute anal-sadistic impulses are just as unacceptable as the abandoned genital interest and are not satisfactory masks. In fact, they are so distasteful and anxiety-provoking in turn that they have to be repressed by means of such repressive defenses as reaction-formation, isolation, and undoing. Thus obsessional neuroses as conceived by Freud involve a first stage of regression and then a repressive-defense reaction to the regressively reactivated pregenital impulses.

Consciousness is only secondarily affected in regression. While it is true that the genital interests that are given up are then absent from awareness, this effect upon consciousness is an incidental by-product of the fact that one drive has replaced another. In regression, substitution of drives is the main mechanism of ego-protection, while in reaction-formation an alteration of the existing, and basically unchanged, drive is made in consciousness as the means of controlling anxiety.

Freud was emphatic in his insistence that regression and repression differ: "I think, however, that I had better warn you now above all not to confound *Regression* with *Repression* and that I must assist you to clear your minds about the relation between the two processes. *Repression,* as you will remember, is the process by which a mental act capable of becoming conscious (that is, one which belongs to the preconscious system) is made unconscious and forced back into the unconscious system. And we also call it *repression* when the unconscious mental act is not permitted to enter the adjacent preconscious system at all, but is turned back upon the threshold by the censorship. . . . what we have . . . called *'regression'* and considered in its relation to fixation signified exclusively the return of *the libido* to its former halting-places [fixation points] in development, that is, something which is essentially quite different from repression and quite independent of it." (1916–17, pp. 299–300.)

SUMMARY

The interaction of force and counterforce that underlies the concept of repression and defense can best be discussed in terms of several general groups of effects that it produces on psychological processes. We may first distinguish a group of ego-protective mechanisms centering around alterations of consciousness. This grouping was never explicitly named by Freud; here the mechanisms are called "repressive defenses." As his psychological theory developed, Freud distinguished new defenses that do not involve alterations of consciousness; although the term is not a satisfactory one, these may be called "nonrepressive defenses."

The contrast between Freud's own formal classification of his terminology in 1926 and his actual usage of "repression" in referring to these various effects is schematically shown on page 37. As indicated in Chapter I, Freud compounded confusion by using "repression" and/or "defense" at one time or another to refer to most of these mechanisms.

The differences between the defenses here called "repressive" and "nonrepressive" may be illustrated by consideration of one of the nonrepressive defenses, regression.

There are two types of regression: a return of interest from mature extrafamilial personal relationships to an incestuous interest in parents (object regression), and a return of sex drive from a genital motive to a pregenital one (drive regression).

In regression to a pregenital drive, the defense mechanism involves the *substitution* of one drive for another. This is in contrast to repressive defenses in which the defensive action involves a conscious *misrepresenta-*

36

REPRESSIVE AND "NONREPRESSIVE" DEFENSES

Defense (All Forms of Ego-Protection against Dangerous Impulses)

1926 Proposal	*Actual Usage*
1. Repression (amnesic forgetting)	1. Repression (repressive defenses)
2. Conversion	a. amnesia
3. Reaction-formation	b. conversion
4. Projection	c. reaction-formation
5. Isolation	d. projection
6. etc.	e. isolation
	f. etc.
	2. "Nonrepressive" defenses
	a. sublimation
	b. regression
	c. "destruction in the id"
	d. condemnation
	e. inhibitions of emotion and behavior
	f. etc.

tion of drive without the underlying drive being actually changed. Regression involves a replacement, repressive defense a superficial disguise.

In the second form of regression the two drives have a developmental relationship to one another. In a repressive defense, the drive that replaces another does not have such a relationship to the drive it replaces. Instead, the replacing drive seems to be chosen purely in terms of its excellence as a disguise for the real drive and for its ego acceptability. In regression the replacing drive may be no more acceptable to the person than the one replaced.

In contrast to the primary role of alteration of consciousness as the ego-protective mechanism in repressive defenses, the alteration of consciousness that takes place in regression is a secondary by-product of the substitution of drives.

Freud himself distinguished sharply between regression and repression. Regression was never called "a form of repression" as were each of the repressive defenses.

Regression was distinguished as a defense at a later point in the history of psychoanalysis than was true of repressive defenses. Its orientation around developmental drive substitution rather than control of consciousness reflects Freud's own progression of interests from the conscious and unconscious in the early days to the development of personality over the life span.

III

⅄. Inhibitory Defenses

As THE theory of repression developed, Freud turned to a consideration of several kinds of inhibitions as protective devices. He said that repression not only worked to keep dangerous material out of consciousness, but also attempted to prevent arousal of the dangerous impulse by directly inhibiting its development as a psychic process within the person, and by keeping the person from undertaking activity that would arouse the impulse:

"It is of especial interest to us to have established the fact that repression can succeed in inhibiting an instinctual impulse from being turned into a manifestation affect. This shows us that the system *Cs.* [the ego] normally controls affectivity as well as access to motility; and it enhances the importance of repression, since it shows that repression results not only in withholding things from consciousness, but also in preventing the development of affect and the setting-off of muscular activity. Conversely, too, we may say that as long as the system *Cs.* controls affectivity and motility, the mental condition of the person in question may be spoken of as normal." (1915c, pp. 178–79.)

These two effects of defense can be called emotional inhibition (or affective inhibition) and behavioral inhibition (or ego-restriction). While Freud calls them "repression," he clearly distinguishes them from repression in the sense of control of conscious representation as the means of ego-protection. In the language adopted herein, affective inhibition and ego-restriction are nonrepressive defenses. They achieve ego-protection by preventing arousal of impulses rather than by distorting the conscious representation of already aroused impulses as in the repressive defenses.

38

EMOTIONAL INHIBITION

In the defense of emotional inhibition ego-protection is achieved by preventing the dangerous inner impulse from developing into an active process. When anger is inhibited, for instance, a person who has been unjustly treated will not feel angry. No emotion develops despite provocation. This is different from becoming angry and distorting one's representation of one's anger by reaction-formation, projection, or displacement in the repressive defenses.

Freud's interest in the emotional aspects of nonrepressive defense was evident as early as 1907: "We remain on the surface so long as we are dealing only with memories and ideas. What is alone of value in mental life is rather the feelings. No mental forces are significant unless they possess the characteristic of arousing feelings. Ideas are only repressed because they are associated with the release of feelings which ought not to occur. It would be more correct to say that repression acts upon feelings, but we can only be aware of these in their association with ideas." (1907, pp. 48–49.)

This emphasis upon the effects of defense in inhibiting emotional development increased in Freud's subsequent writings: "We know, too, that to suppress the development of affect is the true aim of repression and that its work is incomplete if this aim is not achieved. In every instance where repression has succeeded in inhibiting the development of affects, we term those affects (which we restore when we undo the work of repression) 'unconscious'. Thus it cannot be denied that the use of the terms in question is consistent; but in comparison with unconscious ideas there is the important difference that unconscious ideas continue to exist after repression as actual structures in the system *Ucs.*, whereas all that corresponds in that system to unconscious affects is a potential beginning which is prevented from developing." (1915c, p. 178.)

In this quotation, the difference between inhibition and repressive defense is clearly stated by Freud at the point where he says that unconscious ideas continue to exist after repression (that is, they continue as active processes but their conscious representation is distorted), while unconscious affects (inhibited affects) are prevented from developing.

Emotional inhibition is so distinct from repressive defense that the ideational aspects which are involved in repressive defenses can become conscious and be unrepressed, yet the defensive emotional inhibition remains. This condition is found in the defense of negation and in certain phenomena of therapy:

"Thus the subject-matter of a repressed image or thought can make its way into consciousness on condition that it is *denied*. Negation is a way of taking account of what is repressed; indeed, it is actually a removal of the repression, though not, of course, an acceptance of what is repressed. It is to be seen how the intellectual function is here distinct from the affective process. Negation only assists in undoing *one* of the consequences of repression — namely, the fact that the subject-matter of the image in question is unable to enter consciousness. The result is a kind of intellectual acceptance of what is repressed, though in all essentials the repression persists. In the course of analytic work we often bring about a further very important and somewhat bewildering modification of the same situation. We succeed in defeating the negation too and in establishing a complete intellectual acceptance of what is repressed — but the repression itself is still not removed." (1925a, p. 182.)

This quotation shows how confusing Freud's lack of a differentiated terminology can be. It is puzzling to read about the "removal of the repression" and then to be told "the repression persists," until one sees that he is distinguishing between the effect of repression in controlling consciousness (repressive defenses) and the effect of defense in inhibiting emotional development. In negation the control of consciousness has been restored to normal but the requisite emotional experience has not developed.

A similar situation comes about if the therapist simply tells the patient what he is repressing. This undoes the repressive defense, but without a corresponding release of the capacity for emotional development from inhibition a significant part of the defense continues to persist: "If we communicate to a patient some idea which he has at one time repressed but which we have discovered in him, our telling him makes at first no change in his mental condition. Above all, it does not remove the repression nor undo its effects, as might perhaps be expected from the fact that the previously unconscious idea has now become conscious. . . . a moment's reflection shows that the identity of the information given to the patient with his repressed memory is only apparent. To have heard something and to have experienced something are in their psychological nature two quite different things, even though the content of both is the same." (1915c, p. 176.)

Unless one distinguishes between repressive defense and emotional inhibition, this statement is not comprehensible. Indeed, Freud is making this very distinction, but he has not developed a differentiated vocabulary to match his theoretical distinctions. He tries to use "repression" to cover everything.

EGO-RESTRICTION OR BEHAVIORAL INHIBITION

Not only may inhibition be emotional, it may also be behavioral. In ego-restriction, or behavioral inhibition,* the person restricts his activities in such a way as to avoid engaging in any which would arouse dangerous impulses. Little can be said about these "precautionary inhibitions" since, as with affective inhibition, Freud's writings about behavioral inhibitions are relatively meagre as compared with the voluminous treatment of repressive defenses.

Freud did devote the first short chapter in his *Inhibitions, Symptoms and Anxiety* to behavioral inhibitions. There he pointed out various neurotic inhibitions of sexual function, eating, walking, and working (pp. 87–90), and ended with this definition: ". . . inhibition is the *expression of a restriction of an ego-function*" (1926a, p. 89).

In neuroses, such functional limitations occur whenever the activity in question has come unconsciously to mean gratification of dangerous impulse. The inhibitions are precautionary avoidances: "The ego renounces these functions, which are within its sphere, in order not to have to undertake fresh measures of repression — *in order to avoid a conflict with the id*.

"There are clearly also inhibitions which serve the purpose of self-punishment. This is often the case in inhibitions of professional activities. The ego is not allowed to carry on those activities, because they would bring success and gain, and these are things which the severe super-ego has forbidden. So the ego gives them up too, *in order to avoid coming into conflict with the super-ego*." (1926a, p. 90).

Besides these precautionary inhibitions, Freud considered that there were neurotic inhibitions resulting from states (such as mourning) in which the ego was involved in an especially difficult task, such as controlling intense sex or aggression. This great defensive effort leaves the person impoverished in energy so that the ego has to inhibit other activities for lack of energy.

* While "behavioral inhibition" is logically correct and is used herein to call attention to the relationship of this defense to emotional inhibition, "ego-restriction" has come into general use as a name for this defense.

In summary: "As regards inhibitions, then, we may say in conclusion that they are restrictions of the functions of the ego which have been either imposed as a measure of precaution or brought about as a result of an impoverishment of energy" (1926a, p. 90).

SUMMARY

Defenses that achieve ego-protection through inhibition may be recognized as a type of defense separate from repressive defenses, and from "non-repressive" defenses like regression. Emotional inhibition and ego-restriction are two such inhibitory defenses.

In emotional inhibition control of anxiety is achieved by preventing the arousal of impulses within the person. This contrasts with repressive defenses that allow the impulse to develop as an active process but misrepresent its true nature in consciousness. In inhibition emotions do not exist as actual processes; in repressive defense they exist but are disguised.

The distinction between "repressive defenses" and "emotional inhibition" allows an account of therapy in which intellectual acceptance can be achieved without emotional acceptance. Without such a distinction, Freud had to speak of the "removal of the repression" at the same time that he also insisted that "the repression itself is still not removed." With this new terminology one can discuss unambiguously a situation in which a repressive defense is lifted, allowing correct intellectual representation of the impulse, but in which emotional inhibition is continued.

In ego-restriction, which might also be called behavioral inhibition, anxiety is controlled by refusal to participate in activities that would arouse dangerous impulses. Ego-restriction is, along with emotional inhibition, an "inhibitory defense," but differs in that one controls feelings while the other controls behavior.

42

IV

✗. Resistance

IN THE organization of Freud's theory presented in this book, resistances make up one large class of the several main types of manifestation of repression. Resistance is undoubtedly not only the most important indicator of repression, but a key idea in his whole theory.

Freud himself pointed to this special position of resistance and said that repression was the theoretical formulation of the resistance phenomenon: "As you are aware, the whole of psychoanalytic theory is in fact built up on the perception of the resistance exerted by the patient when we try to make him conscious of his unconscious" (1933, p. 97). And again: "The theory of repression . . . is nothing but a theoretical formulation of a phenomenon which may be observed as often as one pleases if one undertakes an analysis of a neurotic without resorting to hypnosis. In such cases one comes across a resistance which opposes the work of analysis and in order to frustrate it pleads a failure of memory." (1914a, p. 16.) Clearly, in resistance we have come to grips with a phenomenon that, as well as being the historical foundation of psychoanalysis, is the heart of the whole theory of repression and defense. What does "resistance" mean? There are a half-dozen major facets to the idea.

RESISTANCE AND REPRESSION
What is the relation of resistance to repression?

It is clear that resistance is a manifestation of the repression tendency: "The pathogenic process which is demonstrated by the resistances we call REPRESSION." (1916–17, pp. 258–259.)

The relation of resistance and repression is that of a specific instance to a general process. "Repression" refers to a wide variety of efforts on the part of the patient to cope with inner impulses that he feels are dangerous. "Resistance" is a term that Freud applied to these protective efforts as seen in the therapeutic situation. It is the therapy-room manifestation of the repression tendency at work: "For the moment, however, we are not concerned with the pathogenic role of the defensive mechanisms. Our purpose is to discover how our therapeutic work is affected by the ego-modifications they produce . . . The main point is that the patient repeats these modes of reaction during analysis itself, exhibiting them, as it were, before our eyes; in fact, that is the only means we have of learning about them . . . The crux of the matter is that the mechanisms of defence against former dangers recur in analysis in the shape of *resistances* to cure. It follows that the ego treats recovery itself as a new danger." (1937, p. 341.) "This action undertaken to protect repression is observable in analytic treatment as *resistance*" (1926a, p. 157).

In this comparison of Freud's, repression shows itself in two forms, first as the process responsible for symptom formation, and in therapy as the same process responsible, now, for resistance: "In what way can we now account for this fact [the fact of resistance] observed, that the patient struggles so energetically against the relief of his symptoms and the restoration of his mental processes to normal functioning? We say that we have come upon the traces of powerful forces at work here opposing any change in the condition; they must be the same forces that originally induced the condition. In the formation of symptoms some process must have been gone through, which our experience in dispersing them makes us able to reconstruct . . . A vehement effort must have been exercised to prevent the mental process in question from penetrating into consciousness and as a result it has remained unconscious; being unconscious it had the power to construct a symptom. The same vehement effort is again at work during analytic treatment opposing the attempt to bring the unconscious into consciousness. This we perceive in the form of resistances. The pathogenic process which is demonstrated by the resistances we call REPRESSION." (1916–17, pp. 258–259.)

Symptom formation and resistance are thus to be considered alternative manifestations of the more general process of repression.

RESISTANCE AS BEHAVIOR

The simplest but in some ways the most fundamental fact is that "resistance" refers to certain types of behavior. The patient in therapy *does* certain things and these seeable, countable actions are indicators at the behavioral level of a repression tendency at work. A large number of examples of such behaviors that Freud specifically pointed to as instances of resistance are given later in this chapter in the section called "Types of Resistance." They include such actions as remaining silent, giving absurd associations, avoiding certain topics, repeating certain themes in an unvarying way. That Freud clearly identified resistance behavior by means of such examples is particularly of interest to research workers who might want to construct measures of repression tendency, since Freud's examples indicate the type of behavior that would be counted or measured.

In observation language, then, "resistance" refers to certain kinds of behavior observable in therapy.

RESISTANCE AS A HYPOTHETICAL FORCE

Resistance refers to behavior, but it also makes an inference about processes that cannot be observed directly. Freud hypothesized about the nature of the events behind resistance behavior and, on the basis of his observation that he as the therapist was exerting a pressure upon his patients that seemed to be opposed by a counter-reaction on their part, he decided that the process behind resistance behavior had the character of a psychological force:

"When, at our first interview, I asked my patients if they remembered what had originally occasioned the symptom concerned, in some cases they said they knew nothing of it, while in others they brought forward something which they described as an obscure recollection and could not pursue further . . . I now became insistent. . . . I told the patients to lie down and deliberately close their eyes in order to 'concentrate'. . . . I then found that without any hypnosis new recollections emerged which went further back. . . . since this insistence involved effort on my part and so suggested the idea that I had to overcome a resistance, the situation led me at once to the theory that *by means of my psychical work I had to overcome a psychical force in the patients which was opposed to the pathogenic ideas becoming conscious (being remembered)*." (1895, p. 268.) "The amount of effort required of the physician varied in different cases; it increased in direct proportion to the difficulty of what had to be remembered. The expenditure of force on the part of the physician was evidently the measure of a *resistance* on the part of the patient." (1925b, p. 29.)

In theoretical language, then, resistance refers to a psychological force in the patient. In its earliest form, Freud conceived it as a force that opposed the therapist's efforts to get the patient to remember the events of his past; later the force was generalized to include *any* opposition to the therapist's efforts to change the patient.

ANTICATHEXIS, RESISTANCE, AND REPRESSION

For a time Freud used "resistance" as the term to cover his concept of the counterforce that opposed the dangerous impulse, as in the following passages: "The resistance too arises in a repression, either from the very one which we are endeavouring to dispel, or in one that occurred earlier. It is set up by the counter-charge which rose up to repress the repellent impulse . . ." (1916–17, p. 379.) But, as we have seen, the term "resistance" was limited to the therapeutic situation, whereas the counter-charge against the repellant wish could work in other situations of the patient's life as well as in therapy. A more general name for this counter-force was needed, a name that could be applied to any of its manifestations. This became increasingly necessary as Freud's thought developed from a theory of therapy to a theory of mental illness and of psychology more generally. He found a more general term in "anticathexis." Resistance is the therapeutic counterpart of anticathexis: "Resistance presupposes the existence of what I have called *anticathexis*" (1926a, p. 157).

Freud formulated the concept of anticathexis in his 1915 paper on "The Unconscious," although he had used the term as early as 1900 in the *Interpretation of Dreams* (1900, p. 605). The relevant passages from "The Unconscious" are complex. It will help the reader to recall that in 1915 Freud had not yet formulated his psychology in terms of ego, id, and superego. Most of what later become ego was called "system Cs." ("Cs." for conscious) and "system Pcs." (preconscious system), and what later become id was referred to as "system Ucs." (unconscious system). Freud is also concerned at this point in the paper with obscure questions of energy relationships between the Cs. and Ucs.

The important point for our present topic is Freud's realization (see the third paragraph of the quotation below) that if the repressed impulse was conceived as exerting a constant pressure toward expression in consciousness and behavior, that impulse ought to keep appearing and thus repression would have to be repeated constantly — the impulse would be like a jack-in-the-box that endlessly popped up and had to be repeatedly

46

pressed down. He suggested that there must be a constant "anti-pressure" that kept the repressed impulse "down," and called it "anticathexis" (paragraph four):

"We have arrived at the conclusion that repression is essentially a process affecting ideas on the border between the systems *Ucs.* and *Pcs.* (*Cs.*), and we can now make a fresh attempt to describe the process in greater detail.

"It must be a matter of a *withdrawal* of cathexis; but the question is, in which system does the withdrawal take place and to which system does the cathexis that is withdrawn belong? The repressed idea remains capable of action in the *Ucs.*, and it must therefore have retained its cathexis. What has been withdrawn must be something else. Let us take the case of repression proper ('after-pressure'), as it affects an idea which is preconscious or even actually conscious. Here repression can only consist in withdrawing from the idea the (pre)conscious cathexis which belongs to the system *Pcs.* The idea then either remains uncathected, or receives cathexis from the *Ucs.*, or retains the *Ucs.* cathexis which it already had. Thus there is a withdrawal of the preconscious cathexis, retention of the unconscious cathexis, or replacement of the preconscious cathexis by an unconscious one. We notice, moreover, that we have based these reflections (as it were, without meaning to) on the assumption that the transition from the system *Ucs.* to the system next to it is not effected through the making of a new registration but through a change in its state, an alteration in its cathexis. The functional hypothesis has here easily defeated the topographical one.

"But this process of withdrawal of libido is not adequate to make another characteristic of repression comprehensible to us. It is not clear why the idea which has remained cathected or has received cathexis from the *Ucs.* should not, in virtue of its cathexis, renew the attempt to penetrate into the system *Pcs.* If it could do so, the withdrawal of libido from it would have to be repeated, and the same performance would go on endlessly; but the outcome would not be repression. So, too, when it comes to describing *primal* repression, the mechanism just discussed of withdrawal of preconscious cathexis would fail to meet the case; for here we are dealing with an unconscious idea which has as yet received *no* cathexis from the *Pcs*, and therefore cannot have that cathexis withdrawn from it.

"What we require, therefore, is another process which maintains the repression in the first case [i.e., the case of after-pressure] and, in the second [i.e., that of primal repression], ensures its being established as well as continued. This other process can only be found in the assumption of an *anticathexis*, by means of which the system *Pcs.* protects itself from the pressure upon it of the unconscious idea. We shall see from clinical examples how such an anticathexis, operating in the system *Pcs.*, manifests itself. It is this which represents the permanent expenditure [of energy] of a primal repression, and which also guarantees the permanence of that repression. Anticathexis is the sole mechanism of primal repression; in the case of repression proper ('after-pressure') there is in addition withdrawal of the *Pcs.* cathexis. It is very possible that it is precisely the cathexis which is withdrawn from the idea that is used for anticathexis." (1915c, pp. 180–81.)

Freud, in other words, now had a general name, "anticathexis," for the counterforce exerted by the repression tendency, a counterforce opposing the tendency of the dangerous impulse to become conscious and to control action. This general counterforce was present in the various repression situations, as when symptoms were formed in the clash between impulse and the anticathectic force, or in childhood repression (primal repression). When the anticathectic or counterimpulse force appeared in the therapeutic situation it was called resistance. Thus resistance as force is a particular type of anticathexis, while anticathexis is the counterforce aspect of repression.

RESISTANCE AS UNCONSCIOUS PROCESS

It should be obvious that resistance as a form of repression is not a conscious process:

"First: when we undertake to cure a patient of his symptoms he opposes against us a vigorous and tenacious *resistance* throughout the entire course of treatment . . . The patient . . . exhibits all the manifestations of this resistance without recognizing it as such, and it is a great step forward when we have brought him to realize this fact and to reckon with it." (1916–17, p. 253.)

VARIATIONS IN RESISTANCE

Resistance behavior is not constant during treatment. It is particularly strong when a new topic is taken up: "In the course of treatment the resistance varies in intensity continually; it always increases as a new topic

48

is approached; it is at its height during the work upon it, and dies down again when this theme has been dealt with" (1916–17, p. 258).

Resistance is also especially strong just preceding interpretations: "Whenever we are on the point of bringing to his [the patient's] consciousness some piece of unconscious material which is particularly painful to him, then he is critical in the extreme; even though he may have previously understood and accepted a great deal, yet now all these gains seem to be obliterated; in his struggles to oppose at all costs he can behave just as though he were mentally deficient, a form of 'emotional stupidity' " (1916–17, p. 258).

The variability of resistance in treatment is an important problem for research workers who try to develop measures of resistance. The measures cannot be taken at just any point in therapy since the theory predicts variation according to such factors as those mentioned.

TYPES OF RESISTANCE

The concept of resistance began with Freud's interpretation of the patient's inability and apparent unwillingness to carry out his agreement to tell everything that came to his mind. The concept grew as the theory of psychoanalysis developed into a complex system of psychology. The most important change in the concept of resistance was its reinterpretation to include what, on the surface, looked like different *types* of behavior during therapy, but were, Freud came to believe, simply varying manifestations of resistance. By 1926 there were five kinds of resistance recognized by Freud:

"Further investigation of the subject shows that the analyst has to combat no less than five kinds of resistance, emanating from three directions — the ego, the id and the super-ego. The ego is the source of three of these, each differing in its dynamic nature. The first of these three ego-resistances is the *repression* resistance, which we have already discussed above . . . and about which there is least new to be added. Next there is the *transference* resistance, which is of the same nature but which has different and much clearer effects in analysis, since it succeeds in establishing a relation to the analytic situation or the analyst himself and thus re-animating a repression which should only have been recollected. The third resistance, though also an ego-resistance, is of quite a different nature. It proceeds from the *gain from illness* and is based upon

49

an assimilation of the symptom into the ego. . . . It represents an unwillingness to renounce any satisfaction or relief that has been obtained. The fourth variety, arising from the *id*, is the resistance which, as we have just seen, necessitates 'working-through'. The fifth, coming from the *super-ego* and the last to be discovered, is also the most obscure though not always the least powerful one. It seems to originate from the sense of guilt or the need for punishment; and it opposes every move towards success, including, therefore, the patient's own recovery through analysis." (1926a, p. 160.)

Repression-Resistance. When Freud began to distinguish among different types of resistance, he gave the name "repression-resistance" to the familiar forms of resistance behavior that had first been identified: "With the mention of resistance we have reached the second and more important part of our task. We have already heard that the ego protects itself against the incursion of undesirable elements from the unconscious and repressed id by means of anti-cathexes, which must remain intact if it is to function normally. The more hardly the ego feels itself pressed, the more convulsively it clings (in terror, as it were) to these anti-cathexes, in order to protect what remains of it from further irruptions. . . . we become aware of the strength of these anti-cathexes in the form of *resistances* against our work. The ego shrinks from undertakings that seem dangerous and threaten unpleasure. . . . This resistance, which persists through the whole treatment and is renewed with every fresh piece of work, has been named, though not quite correctly, *repression-resistance*." (1940, pp. 72–73.)

While repression-resistance includes a broad variety of avoidance behavior it centers particularly around the patient's attempts to evade the requirement that he tell everything that comes to mind in free association: "The first thing that happens as a result of instituting this technical rule [the requirement of saying everything that comes to one's mind] is that it becomes the first point of attack for the resistance. The patient attempts to escape from it by every possible means. First he says nothing comes into his head, then that so much comes into his head that he can't grasp any of it. Then we observe with displeasure and astonishment that he is giving in to his critical objections, first to this, then to that; he betrays it by the long pauses which occur in his talk. At last he admits that he really cannot say something, he is ashamed to, and he lets this feeling get the better of his promise. Or else, he has thought of something but it concerns someone else and not himself, and is therefore to be made an exception to the rule. Or else, what he has just thought of is really too unimportant, too stupid and too absurd, I could never have meant that he should take account of such thoughts. So it goes on, with untold variations, to which one continually replies that telling everything really means telling everything." (1916–17, p. 254.)

General accounts of repression-resistance such as that just quoted, many other specific discussions, and, often, unelaborated hints, yield a large number of particular forms that repression-resistance can take. A few examples from Freud follow.

1. Making mental reservations to exempt certain information from the fundamental rule: "One hardly ever meets with a patient who does not attempt to make a reservation in some department of his thoughts, in order to guard against intrusion by the analysis. One patient, who in the ordinary way was remarkably intelligent, concealed a most intimate love-affair from me for weeks in this way; when accused of this violation of the sacred rule he defended himself with the argument that he considered this particular story his private affair. Naturally analytic treatment cannot countenance a right of sanctuary like this." (1916–17, p. 254.)

2. Associative blocks: "The objective indication of resistance is that his associations stop short" (1933, p. 97).

3. Absurd associations: "Patients with anxiety-hysteria [phobia] some-times succeed in reducing it [the technical rule] to absurdity by only pro-ducing associations which are so far removed from what is wanted that they yield nothing for analysis" (1916–17, p. 255). This displacement from a normal and serious association to apparently absurd ones is also discussed by Freud in his book on interpretation of dreams (1900, pp. 530–31).

4. Associative avoidance: "The objective indication of resistance is that [the patient's] associations . . . wander far away from the theme that is being discussed" (1933, p. 97). "We showed on an earlier occasion that the resistance that has to be overcome in analysis proceeds from the ego, which clings to its anticathexes. It is hard for the ego to direct its attention to perceptions and ideas which it has up till now made a rule of avoiding, or to acknowledge as belonging to itself impulses that are the complete opposite of those which it knows as its own." (1926a, p. 159.)

In the Dora case Freud found that he had great difficulty at first in getting her to talk about Herr K., which turned out to be the main emotional issue in the therapy: "I did not find it easy, however, to direct the patient's attention to her relations with Herr K. She declared that she had done with him." (1905b, p. 32.)

5. Manifest intellectual opposition to the theory of psychoanalysis: ". . . finally, with resolution and perseverance, we do succeed in extracting from the patient a certain amount of obedience for the rule of the technique; and then the resistance takes another line altogether. It appears as intellectual opposition, employs arguments as weapons, and turns to its own use all the difficulties and improbabilities which normal but uninstructed reasoning finds in analytical doctrines. We then have to hear from the mouth of the individual patient all the criticisms and objections which thunder about us in chorus in scientific literature." (1916–17, p. 255.)

6. Manifestly expressed interest in being instructed in the theory of psychoanalysis by the analyst: "[The patient] is very glad to get us to instruct him, teach him, defeat him, point out the literature to him so that he can learn more; he is perfectly ready to become a supporter of psychoanalysis on the condition that analysis shall spare him personally. We recognize resistance in this desire for knowledge, however; it is a digression from the particular task in hand and we refuse to allow it." (1916–17, p. 255.)

7. Concealed reservation of doubt as to the validity of psychoanalysis: "In the obsessional neurosis the resistance makes use of special tactics which we are prepared for. It permits the analysis to proceed uninterruptedly along its course, so that more and more light is thrown upon the problems of the case, until we begin to wonder at last why these explanations have no practical effect and entail no corresponding improvement in the symptoms. Then we discover that the resistance has fallen back upon the doubt characteristic of the obsessional neurosis and is holding us successfully at bay from this vantage-point. The patient has said to himself something of this kind: 'This is all very pretty and very interesting. I should like to go on with it. I am sure it would do me a lot of good if it were true. But I don't believe it in the least, and as long as I don't believe it, it doesn't affect my illness." (1916–17, pp. 255–56.)

8. Making use of accidental occurrences to delay therapy: "Besides this, you must take into account that all accidental occurrences arising during the treatment are made use of by the patient to interfere with it,

anything which could distract him or deter him from it, every hostile expression of opinion from anyone in his circle whom he can regard as an authority, any chance organic illness or one complicating the neurosis; indeed, he even converts every improvement in his condition into a motive for slackening his efforts" (1916–17, p. 257).

Earlier Freud had written: "Psychoanalysis is justly suspicious. One of its rules is that *whatever* interrupts the progress of analytic work is a resistance." (1900, p. 517.) In 1925 he added a footnote to this sentence: "The proposition laid down in these peremptory terms — 'whatever interrupts the progress of analytic work is a resistance' — is easily open to misunderstanding. . . . It cannot be disputed that in the course of an analysis various events may occur the responsibility for which cannot be laid upon the patient's intentions . . . But behind its obvious exaggeration the proposition is asserting something both true and new. Even if the interrupting event is a real one and independent of the patient, it often depends on him how great an interruption it causes; and resistance shows itself unmistakably in the readiness with which he accepts an occurrence of this kind or the exaggerated use which he makes of it."

9. Expressions of doubt about the correctness of details in past happenings, or of details in dreams: "If a patient exhibits doubts in the course of his narrative, an empirical rule teaches us to disregard such expressions of his judgement entirely. If the narrative wavers between two versions, we should incline to regard the first one as correct and the second as a product of repression." (1905b, p. 17, footnote 2.)

In *The Interpretation of Dreams* Freud makes the same suggestion about doubt in relation to details of dreams (1900, p. 515). In a footnote on pp. 517–18 he gives a concrete example of a patient who was in doubt about the element "channel" in her dream.

10. Changes in details of dreams on second telling: "In analysing the dreams of my patients I sometimes put this assertion to the following test, which has never failed me. If the first account given me by a patient of a dream is too hard to follow I ask him to repeat it. In doing so he rarely uses the same words. But the parts of the dream which he describes in different terms are by that fact revealed to me as the weak spot in the dream's disguise . . . My request to the patient to repeat his account of the dream has warned him that I was proposing to take special pains in solving it; under pressure of the resistance, therefore, he hastily covers the weak spots in the dream's disguise by replacing any expressions that

threaten to betray its meaning by other less revealing ones." (1900, p. 515.)

A concrete example of such alteration on repetition is given in the Dora case where Dora changed "two and a half hours" to "two hours" upon repetition of the dream (1905b, footnote to p. 94).

11. The forgetting of details of dreams and past events: "The *forgetting* of dreams, too, remains inexplicable unless the power of the psychical censorship is taken into account . . . It is often possible by means of analysis to restore all that has been lost by the forgetting of the dream's content . . . [this] shows that there was no lack of a hostile [i.e. resistant] purpose at work in the forgetting of the dream." (1900, p. 517, translator's brackets.)

Forgetting life-history events is, of course, one of the classical signs of resistance. A specific discussion is found in the Dora case: "[In the patient's history] there are invariably true amnesias — gaps in the memory into which not only old recollections but even quite recent ones have fallen — and paramnesias, formed secondarily so as to fill in those gaps. When the events themselves have been kept in mind, the purpose underlying the amnesias can be fulfilled just as surely by destroying a connection, and a connection is most surely broken by altering the chronological order of events. The latter always proves to be the most vulnerable element in the store of memory and the one which is most easily subject to repression. Again, we meet with many recollections that are in what might be described as the first stage of repression, and these we find surrounded with doubts. At a later period the doubts would be replaced by a loss or a falsification of memory." (1905b, p. 17.)

Vagueness about past history or details of dreams has the same status as forgetting as a sign of resistance.

12. Monotonous repetition of certain themes: Instead of talking about her real problem, which had to do with her relation to Herr K., Dora persistently castigated her father. "I did not find it easy, however, to direct the patient's attention to her relations with Herr K. She declared that she had done with him. The uppermost layer of all her associations during the sessions, and everything of which she was easily conscious and of which she remembered having been conscious the day before, was always connected with her father." (1905b, p. 32.) Referring to Dora's unvarying reproaches against her father, Freud continued: "But it soon becomes evident that the patient is using thoughts of this kind . . . for

54

the purpose of cloaking others which are anxious to escape from criticism and from consciousness" (1905b, p. 35).

13. Subjective feelings of unpleasure: "On the other side there are fighting against us the negative transference, the ego's repression-resistance (that is, the unpleasure felt by it at undertaking the severe work imposed upon it)" (1940, p. 77).

Transference-Resistance. The most important, and in some ways most radical, expansion of the resistance concept was Freud's interpretation of transference as a form of resistance: "But the patient knows how to set up resistances within the boundaries of analysis proper, and the defeat of these is one of the most difficult tasks of the technique. Instead of remembering certain of the feelings and states of mind of his previous life, he reproduces them, lives through again such of them as, by means of what is called 'transference', may be made effective in opposition against the physician and the treatment." (1916–17, p. 256.) "Next there is the *transference* resistance, which is of the same nature but which has different and much clearer effects in analysis, since it succeeds in establishing a relation to the analytic situation or the analyst himself and thus reanimating a repression which should only have been recollected" (1926a, p. 160). And ". . . in analysis transference emerges as *the most powerful resistance* to the treatment" (1912a, p. 101).

Transference-resistance is not present at the outset of treatment. Freud felt that it developed only after the various types of repression-resistance described in the preceding section had been tried by the patient and been given up under the impact of the analyst's interpretations of them. As these first forms came to offer increasingly less protection, the patient began to develop the already existing relationship to the analyst into a new means of expressing resistance:

"The longer an analytic treatment lasts and the more clearly the patient realizes that distortions of the pathogenic material cannot by themselves offer any protection against its being uncovered, the more consistently does he make use of the one sort of distortion which obviously affords him the greatest advantages — distortion through transference. These circumstances tend towards a situation in which finally every conflict has to be fought out in the sphere of transference.

"Thus transference in the analytic treatment invariably appears to us in the first instance as the strongest weapon of the resistance, and we may conclude that the intensity and persistence of the transference are an effect and an expression of the resistance. The *mechanism* of transference is, it is true, dealt with when we have traced it back to the state of readiness of the libido, which has remained in possession of infantile imagos; but the part transference plays in the treatment can only be explained if we enter into its relations with resistance." (1912a, p. 104.)

A general picture of this concept and of the status of transference as a form of resistance is contained in Chapter 27 of *A General Introduction to Psychoanalysis*. The central passages are the following:

"We observe then that the patient, who ought to be thinking of nothing but the solution of his own distressing conflicts, begins to develop a particular interest in the person of the physician. Everything connected with this person seems to him more important than his own affairs and to distract him from his illness. Relations with the patient then become for a time very agreeable; he is particularly docile, endeavours to show his gratitude wherever he can, exhibits a fineness of character and other good qualities which we had perhaps not anticipated in him. The analyst thus forms a very good opinion of the patient and values his luck in being able to render assistance to such an admirable personality. If the physician has occasion to see the patient's relatives he hears with satisfaction that this esteem is mutual. The patient at home is never tired of praising the analyst and attributing new virtues to him. 'He has quite lost his head over you; he puts implicit trust in you; everything you say is like a revelation to him,' say the relatives. Here and there one among this chorus having sharper eyes will say: 'It is positively boring the way he never speaks of anything but you: he quotes you all the time.'

"We will hope that the physician is modest enough to ascribe the patient's estimate of his value to the hopes of recovery which he has been able to offer to him, and to the widening in the patient's intellectual horizon consequent upon the surprising revelations entailed by the treatment and their liberating influence. The analysis too makes splendid progress under these conditions, the patient understands the suggestions offered to him, concentrates upon the tasks appointed by the treatment, the material needed — his recollections and associations — is abundantly available; he astonishes the analyst by the sureness and accuracy of his interpretations, and the latter has only to observe with satisfaction how readily and willingly a sick man will accept all the new psychological ideas that are so hotly contested by the healthy in the world outside. A general improvement in the patient's condition, objectively confirmed on all sides, also accompanies this harmonious relationship in the analysis.

"But such fair weather cannot last for ever. There comes a day when it clouds over. There begin to be difficulties in the analysis; the patient says he cannot think of anything more to say. One has an unmistakable impression that he is no longer interested in the work, and that he is casually ignoring the injunction given him to say everything that comes into his mind and to yield to none of the critical objections that occur to him. His behaviour is not dictated by the situation of the treatment; it is as if he had not made an agreement to that effect with the physician; he is obviously preoccupied with something which at the same time he wishes to reserve to himself. This is a situation in which the treatment is in danger. Plainly a very powerful resistance has risen up. What can have happened?" (1916–17, pp. 381–82.)

"The new fact which we are thus unwillingly compelled to recognize we call TRANSFERENCE. By this we mean a transference of feelings on to the person of the physician, because we do not believe that the situation in the treatment can account for the origin of such feelings. We are much more disposed to suspect that the whole of this readiness to develop feeling originates in another source; that it was previously formed in the patient, and has seized the opportunity provided by the treatment to transfer itself on to the person of the physician. The transference can express itself as a passionate petitioning for love, or it can take less extreme forms; where a young girl and an elderly man are concerned, instead of the wish to be wife or mistress, a wish to be adopted as a favourite daughter may come to light, the libidinous desire can modify itself and propose itself as a wish for an everlasting, but ideally platonic friendship. Many women understand how to sublimate the transference and to mould it, until it acquires a sort of justification of its existence; others have to express it in its crude, original, almost impossible form. But at bottom it is always the same, and its origin in the same source can never be mistaken.

"Before we enquire where we are to range this new fact, we will amplify the description of it a little. How is it with our male patients? There at least we might hope to be spared the troublesome element of sex difference and sex attraction. Well, the answer is very much the same as with women. The same attachment to the physician, the same overestimation of his qualities, the same adoption of his interests, the same jealousy against all those connected with him. The sublimated kinds of transference are the

57

forms more frequently met with between man and man, and the directly sexual declaration more rarely, in the same degree to which the manifest homosexuality of the patient is subordinated to the other ways by which this component-instinct can express itself. Also, it is in male patients that the analyst more frequently observes a manifestation of the transference which at the first glance seems to controvert the description of it just given — that is, the hostile or *negative* transference.

"First of all, let us realize at once that the transference exists in the patient from the beginning of the treatment, and is for a time the strongest impetus in the work. Nothing is seen of it and one does not need to trouble about it as long as its effect is favourable to the work in which the two persons are co-operating. When it becomes transformed into a resistance, attention must be paid to it; and then it appears that two different and contrasting states of mind have supervened in it and have altered its attitude to the treatment: first, when the affectionate attraction has become so strong and betrays signs of its origin in sexual desire so clearly that it was bound to arouse an inner opposition against itself; and secondly, when it consists in antagonistic instead of affectionate feeling." (1916–17, pp. 384–85.)

There are several more technical aspects of the concept of transference as a form of resistance that are discussed by Freud in two papers devoted to the topic. One question has to do with how it is that transference can function as a resistance, and a second one is whether *all* forms of transference are to be counted as resistance.

In his 1912 paper on "The Dynamics of Transference," Freud asked why it is that ". . . transference emerges as *the most powerful resistance* to the treatment . . ." (1912a, p. 101). He provided two reasons.

First, the transference relation is based on regressively aroused infantile motives. The regression has been brought about by frustrations in the outer world. The same psychological forces which brought about the regression manifest themselves as transference-resistances in treatment: "Where the investigations of analysis come upon the libido withdrawn into its hiding-place, a struggle is bound to break out; all the forces which have caused the libido to regress will rise up as 'resistances' against the work of analysis, in order to conserve the new state of things" (1912a, p. 102).

Second, those parts of personality that are already unconscious exercise an attraction on these regressed aspects of the person, a force in the direc-

58

tion of keeping them as a part of the unconscious complexes: "The libido at the disposal of the subject's personality had always been under the influence of the attraction of his unconscious complexes (or, more correctly, of the portions of those complexes belonging to the unconscious), and it entered on a regressive course because the attraction of reality had diminished. In order to liberate it, this attraction of the unconscious has to be overcome; that is, the repression of the unconscious instincts and of their productions, which has meanwhile been set up in the subject, must be removed. This is responsible for by far the largest part of the resistance, which so often causes the illness to persist even after the turning away from reality has lost its temporary justification." (1912a, p. 103.)

Are all types of transference to be counted as forms of resistance? The answer seems to be that *negative* transference is always to be considered as resistance but that *positive* transference is a form of resistance only when it contains unconscious sexual elements:

"We find in the end that we cannot understand the employment of transference as resistance so long as we think simply of 'transference'. We must make up our minds to distinguish a 'positive' transference from a 'negative' one, the transference of affectionate feelings from that of hostile ones, and to treat the two sorts of transference to the doctor separately. Positive transference is then further divisible into transference of friendly or affectionate feelings which are admissible to consciousness and transference of prolongations of those feelings into the unconscious. . . .

"Thus the solution of the puzzle is that transference to the doctor is suitable for resistance to the treatment only in so far as it is a negative transference or a positive transference of repressed erotic impulses. If we 'remove' the transference by making it conscious, we are detaching only these two components of the emotional act from the person of the doctor; the other component, which is admissible to consciousness and unobjectionable, persists and is the vehicle of success in psychoanalysis exactly as it is in other methods of treatment." (1912a, p. 105.)

In "Observations on Transference-Love" (1915) Freud discusses the use of positive transference as resistance by women patients. The process is one of the usual affectionate feelings (nonresistance positive transference) giving way to a manifest declaration of sexual love for the analyst: "First and foremost, one keeps in mind the suspicion that anything that interferes with the continuation of the treatment may be an expression of resistance. There can be no doubt that the outbreak of a passionate demand for love is largely the work of resistance. One will have long since noticed in the patient the signs of an affectionate transference, and one will have been able to feel certain that her docility, her acceptance of the analytic explanations, her remarkable comprehension and the high degree of intelligence she showed were to be attributed to this attitude towards her doctor. Now all this is swept away. She has become quite without insight and seems to be swallowed up in her love. Moreover, this change quite regularly occurs precisely at a point of time when one is having to try to bring her to admit or remember some particularly distressing and heavily repressed piece of her life-history. She has been in love, therefore, for a long time; but now the resistance is beginning to make use of her love in order to hinder the continuation of the treatment, to deflect all her interest from the work and to put the analyst in an awkward position. . . . She is thus bringing out a resistance under the guise of being in love with him; and in addition to this she has no compunction in placing him in a cleft stick. For if he refuses her love, as his duty and his understanding compel him to do, she can play the part of a woman scorned, and then withdraw from his therapeutic efforts out of revenge and resentment, exactly as she is now doing out of her ostensible love." (1915d, pp. 162–63, 167.)

Male transference-resistance was described by Freud as follows: "If the patient is a man, he usually takes his material from his relationship with his father, in whose place he has now put the physician; and in so doing he erects resistances out of his struggles to attain to personal independence and independence of judgement, out of his ambition, the earliest aim of which was to equal or to excel the father, out of his disinclination to take the burden of gratitude upon himself for the second time in his life. There are periods in which one feels the patient's desire to put the analyst in the wrong, to make him feel his impotence, to triumph over him, has completely ousted the worthier desire to bring the illness to an end." (1916–17, p. 256.)

The radical feature of Freud's interpretation of transference as resistance lies particularly in his assumption that the emotional relationships of the patient to the physician are defensive substitutes for another process which would naturally have occurred except for the patient's ego-protective needs. If defense were not involved, Freud believed, the

60

patient would *remember* the past emotional relationship of his childhood: "Instead of remembering certain of the feelings and states of mind of his previous life, he reproduces them." "*Transference* resistance . . . succeeds in . . . re-animating a repression which should only have been recollected."

Resistance from the Gain of Illness. The third form of ego-resistance comes from the various motivational advantages that being ill bring to the patient. He is unwilling to give up the satisfactions incident to being sick, even though he may also want to get well:

"The third resistance, though also an ego-resistance, is of quite a different nature. It proceeds from the *gain from illness* and is based upon an assimilation of the symptom into the ego. It represents an unwillingness to renounce any satisfaction or relief that has been obtained." (1926a, p. 160.)

"It is therefore only natural that the ego should try to prevent symptoms from remaining isolated and alien by using every possible method to bind them to itself in one way or another, and to incorporate them into its organization by means of these bonds. . . .

"The ego now proceeds to behave as though it recognized that the symptom had come to stay and that the only thing to do was to accept the situation in good part and draw as much advantage from it as possible. It makes an adaptation to the symptom — to this piece of the internal world which is alien to it — just as it normally does to the real external world. It can always find plenty of opportunities for doing so. The presence of a symptom may entail a certain impairment of capacity, and this can be exploited to appease some demand on the part of the super-ego or to refuse some claim from the external world. In this way the symptom gradually comes to be the representative of important interests; it is found to be useful in asserting the position of the self and becomes more and more closely merged with the ego and more and more indispensable to it. . . .

"All of this results in what is familiar to us as the '(secondary) gain from illness' which follows a neurosis. This gain comes to the assistance of the ego in its endeavour to incorporate the symptom and increases the symptom's fixation. When the analyst tries subsequently to help the ego in its struggle against the symptom, he finds that these conciliatory bonds between ego and symptom operate on the side of the resistances and that they are not easy to loosen." (1926a, pp. 98–100.)

Freud further discussed the secondary gain of illness in detail in the Dora case (1950b, pp. 42–46) in a section too long to reproduce here. In those pages he repeats the essence of the quotations given above and explicitly points out that the motives of illness are *unconscious* (p. 45) and the patient is very resistive to recognizing them. It is clear, therefore, that repression is involved and that resistance to recognizing the gain of illness is an index to repression of the motives involved in the illness. In Dora's case, Freud said the motive for being ill ". . . was clearly to touch her father's heart and to detach him from Frau K." (1905b, p. 46).

In his *General Introduction to Psychoanalysis* Freud gives an example of secondary advantage through illness and provides a further descriptive account of the concept:

"But let us continue our discussion without regard to these exceptional cases. In the ordinary way it is apparent that by flight into neurosis the ego gains a certain internal *'advantage through illness,'* as we call it; under certain conditions a tangible external advantage, more or less valuable in reality, may be combined with this. To take the commonest case of this kind: a woman who is brutally treated and mercilessly exploited by her husband fairly regularly takes refuge in a neurosis, if her disposition admits of it. This will happen if she is too cowardly or too conventional to console herself secretly with another man, if she is not strong enough to defy all external reasons against it and separate from her husband, if she has no prospect of being able to maintain herself or of finding a better husband, and last of all, if she is still strongly attached sexually to this brutal man. Her illness becomes her weapon in the struggle against him, one that she can use for her protection, or misuse for purposes of revenge. She can complain of her illness, though she probably dare not complain of her marriage; her doctor is her ally; the husband who is otherwise so ruthless is required to spare her, to spend money on her, to grant her absence from home and thus some freedom from marital oppression. Whenever this external or 'accidental' advantage through illness is at all pronounced, and no substitute for it can be found in reality, you need not look forward very hopefully to influencing the neurosis by your therapy. . . .

"If, as physicians, you have much to do with neurotics, you will soon cease to expect that those who complain most bitterly of their illness will be most ready to accept your help and make least difficulty — quite the contrary. You will at all events easily understand that everything which contributes to the advantage through illness reinforces the resistance arising from the repressions, and increases the therapeutic difficulties. And there is yet another kind of advantage through illness, one which supervenes later than that born with the symptom, so to speak. When such a mental organization as the disease has persisted for a considerable time it seems finally to acquire the character of an independent entity; it displays something like a self-preservative instinct; it forms a kind of pact, a *modus vivendi*, with the other forces in mental life, even with those fundamentally hostile to it, and opportunities can hardly fail to arise in which it once more manifests itself as useful and expedient, thus acquiring a secondary function which again strengthens its position. Instead of taking an example from pathology let us consider a striking illustration in everyday life. A capable working-man earning his living is crippled by an accident in the course of his employment; he can work no more, but he gets a small periodical dole in compensation and learns how to exploit his mutilation as a beggar. His new life, although so inferior, nevertheless is supported by the very thing which destroyed his old life; if you were to remove his disability you would deprive him for a time of his means of subsistence, for the question would arise whether he would still be capable of resuming his former work. When a secondary exploitation of the illness such as this is formed in a neurosis we can range it alongside the first and call it a '*secondary* advantage through illness.'" (1916–17, pp. 333–34.)

Resistance of the Unconscious and Resistance from a Sense of Guilt. These are the fourth and fifth varieties of resistance in Freud's 1926 classification: "The fourth variety, arising from the *id*, is the resistance which, as we have just seen, necessitates 'working through'. The fifth, coming from the *super-ego* and the last to be discovered, is also the most obscure though not always the least powerful one. It seems to originate from the sense of guilt or the need for punishment; and it opposes every move towards success, including, therefore, the patient's own recovery through analysis." (1926a, p. 160.)

It is very difficult to achieve a clear conception of these two further forms of resistance. In his *Outline of Psychoanalysis* written in 1938, Freud grouped them together as sharing in common a "need to be ill" or "need to suffer": "The further our work proceeds and the deeper our knowledge of the mental life of neurotics penetrates, the more clearly two new factors force themselves upon our notice which demand the closest attention as sources of resistance. Both of them are completely unknown to the patient . . . nor do they arise from the patient's ego. They can both be included under the one description of 'need to be ill' or 'need to suffer'; but they are of different origins, though in other respects of a similar nature." (1940, pp. 74–75.)

At times these two forms of resistance are not easy to distinguish from Freud's account of them, and even after close study no very clear picture can be given the reader. An assemblage of relevant quotations for each of these two forms of resistance is provided below.

The first quotation bearing on resistance from a sense of guilt follows directly upon the one reproduced above, in which Freud grouped the two new forms of resistance as sharing in common a "need to be ill": "The first of these two factors is the sense of guilt or consciousness of guilt, as it is called in disregard of the fact that the patient does not feel it and is not aware of it. It is evidently the portion of the resistance contributed by a superego that has grown peculiarly severe and cruel. The patient must not be healthy, he must remain ill, for he deserves no better. This resistance does not actually interfere with our intellectual work, but it makes it ineffective; indeed, it often allows us to remove one form of neurotic suffering but is ready to replace it at once by another one, or perhaps by an organic illness. The sense of guilt also offers an explanation of the cure or improvement of severe neuroses we sometimes observe after real accidents: all that matters is that the patient should be wretched – in what way is of no consequence. The uncomplaining resignation with which such people often put up with their hard fate is most remarkable but also most revealing." (1940, pp. 74–75.)

"There are certain people who behave in a quite peculiar fashion during the work of analysis. When one speaks hopefully to them or expresses satisfaction with the progress of the treatment, they show signs of discontent and their condition invariably becomes worse. One begins by regarding this as defiance and as an attempt to prove their superiority to the physician, but later one comes to take a deeper and truer view. One becomes convinced, not only that such people cannot endure any praise or appreciation, but that they react inversely to the progress of the treatment. Every partial solution that ought to result, and in other people does result, in an improvement or a temporary suspension of symptoms produces in them for the time being an exacerbation of their illness; they get worse during the treatment instead of getting better. They exhibit the so-called negative therapeutic reaction.

"There is no doubt that there is something in these people that sets itself

64

against their recovery and dreads its approach as though it were a danger. We are accustomed to say that the need for illness has got the upper hand in them over the desire for health. If we analyse this resistance in the usual way — then, even after we have subtracted from it the defiant attitude towards the physician and the fixation on the various kinds of advantage which the patient derives from the illness, the greater part of it is still left over; and this reveals itself as the most powerful of all obstacles to recovery, more powerful even than such familiar ones as narcissistic inaccessibility, the assumption of a negative attitude towards the physician or a clinging to the advantages of the illness.

"In the end we come to see that we are dealing with what may be called a 'moral' factor, a sense of guilt, which is finding atonement in the illness and is refusing to give up the penalty of suffering. We are justified in regarding this rather disheartening explanation as conclusive. But as far as the patient is concerned this sense of guilt is dumb; it does not tell him he is guilty; he does not feel guilty, he simply feels ill. This sense of guilt expresses itself only as a resistance to recovery which it is extremely difficult to overcome. It is also particularly difficult to convince the patient that this motive lies behind his continuing to be ill; he holds fast to the more obvious explanation that treatment by analysis is not the right remedy for his case." (1923, pp. 70–72.)

The resistance from a sense of guilt was ascribed by Freud to the working of the aggressive instinct: "In yet another group of cases the patients' resistance to analysis and the obstacles in the way of therapeutic success are probably due to variations in the ego which spring from another and even deeper root. Here we come to the ultimate phenomena to which psychological research has penetrated — the behaviour of the two primal instincts, their distribution, fusion and defusion, things which we cannot imagine to be confined to a single province of the mental apparatus, whether it be id, ego or super-ego. Nothing impresses us more strongly in connection with the resistances encountered in analysis than the feeling that there is a force at work which is defending itself by all possible means against recovery and is clinging tenaciously to illness and suffering. We have recognized that part of this force is the sense of guilt and the need for punishment, and that is undoubtedly correct; we have localized it in the ego's relation to the super-ego. But this is only one element in it, which may be described as psychically bound by the super-ego and which we thus perceive. We may suppose that other portions of the same force are at work, either bound or free, in some unspecified region of the mind. If we consider the whole picture made up of the phenomena of the masochism inherent in so many people, of the negative therapeutic reaction and of the neurotic's sense of guilt, we shall have to abandon the belief that mental processes are governed exclusively by a striving after pleasure. These phenomena are unmistakable indications of the existence of a power in mental life which, according to its aim, we call the aggressive or destructive instinct and which we derive from the primal death-instinct of animate matter. It is not a question of an optimistic as opposed to a pessimistic theory of life. Only by the concurrent or opposing action of the two primal instincts — Eros and the death-instinct — never by one or the other alone, can the motley variety of vital phenomena be explained." (1937, pp. 345–46.)

Resistance of the unconscious is by far the most obscure form of resistance. It shares with resistance from a sense of guilt the tendency toward self-punishment. In the quotation below Freud's description reads very like his description of resistance from a sense of guilt even though it is certain from the context that he is describing resistance of the unconscious: "It is not so easy to demonstrate the existence of yet another form of resistance, our means of combatting which are especially inadequate. There are some neurotics in whom, to judge by all their reactions, the instinct of self-preservation has actually been reversed. They seem to have nothing in view but self-injury and self-destruction. It is possible that people who in the end do in fact commit suicide belong to this group. It must be supposed that in such people far-reaching defusions of instinct have taken place, as a result of which there have been set free excessive quantities of the destructive instinct directed inwards. These patients cannot tolerate the possibility of being cured by our treatment and fight against it with all their force." (1940, pp. 75–76.)

In the description quoted next Freud attributes resistance of the unconscious to, first, the innate tendency of psychic processes to *repeat* themselves, a tendency which is at the basis of the "death instinct" in his theory; and, second, the tendency of unconscious processes to act as a kind of magnet that draws other similar processes, which would normally be conscious, into the unconscious. "For we find that even after the ego has decided to relinquish its resistances it still has difficulty in undoing the repressions; and we have called the period of strenuous effort which follows after its praiseworthy decision, the phase of 'working-through'. The dynamic factor which makes a working-through of this kind necessary and comprehensible is not far to seek. It must be that after the ego-resistance has been removed the power of the compulsion to repeat — the attraction exerted by the unconscious prototypes upon the repressed instinctual process — has still to be overcome. There is nothing to be said against describing this factor as the *resistance of the unconscious*." (1926a, pp. 159–60.)

A final description from one of Freud's last papers identifies resistance of the unconscious with a loss of plasticity: "In another group of patients we are surprised by an attitude which we can only put down to a loss of the plasticity we should expect, an exhaustion of the capacity for change and development. We are indeed prepared for a certain degree of psychical inertia in analysis; when new paths are pointed out for the instinctual impulses, we almost invariably see an obvious hesitation in entering upon them. We have described this attitude, though perhaps not quite rightly, as 'resistance from the id'. But in the cases which I have in mind all the mental processes, relations and distributions of energy are immutable, fixed and rigid. One finds the same state of affairs in very old people, when it is explained by what is described as force of habit, the exhaustion of receptivity through a kind of psychical entropy; but I am thinking of people who are still young. Our theoretical knowledge does not seem adequate to explain these types. Probably some element of a temporal nature is at work here, changes in some rhythm in the development of psychical life which we have not yet apprehended." (1937, p. 345.)

This form of resistance is hard to grasp, particularly because it does not seem to have any identifiable behavioral correlate other than the fact that no change occurs in therapy. The tendency to self-injury could be offered as one such observable behavioral indicator of resistance of the unconscious, but such self-injuring tendencies are also behavioral correlates of resistance from a sense of guilt. The tendency to repeat, the tendency for unconscious processes to attract conscious material to them, and the loss of plasticity do not have behavioral indicators independent of the fact that the person stubbornly keeps on with his old habits and does not change.

RESISTANCE DUE TO "ADHESIVENESS OF THE LIBIDO"?

In his 1937 paper on "Analysis Terminable and Interminable" Freud discussed resistance from a sense of guilt and resistance from the id but seemed to bring up a further form of resistance to which he did not attach a name, or clearly say whether he considered this resistance separate from the other two: "When we advance a step further in analytic experience we come upon resistances of another type, which we can no longer localize and which seem to be conditioned by certain fundamental characteristics of the mental apparatus. I can give only a few examples of the type of resistance to which I refer; this whole field of inquiry is still bewilderingly strange and has not been sufficiently explored. We come across people, for instance, of whom we should say that they display a peculiar 'adhesiveness of libido'. The processes which their analysis sets in motion are so much slower than in other people because they apparently cannot make up their minds to detach libidinal cathexes from one object and displace them to another, although we can find no particular reasons for this cathectic fidelity. Then we meet the opposite type, in which libido seems specially mobile: it readily enters upon the new cathexes suggested by the analysis, abandoning its former ones for these. The difference between the two types is comparable to that experienced by a sculptor according as he works in hard stone or soft clay. Unfortunately in the latter type the results of analysis often prove very evanescent; the new cathexes are soon abandoned and one feels not as if one had been working in clay but as if one had been writing on water. *'Wie gewonnen, so zerronnen'*, as the proverb says." (1937, pp. 344–45.)

This description sounds much like the "loss of plasticity" which Freud described as an aspect of resistance of the unconscious. Perhaps by 1937 he had about decided to separate this element and consider it an independent form of resistance. It is one of those many points left unexplained by Freud, perhaps a half-finished thought which he never returned to.

SUMMARY

Since repression was considered by Freud to be the cornerstone of the psychoanalytic theory, resistance in turn occupies a key place, for Freud regarded repression in its most basic sense as a theoretical formulation of the phenomenon of resistance as seen in therapy. On the most general level, "resistance" is the name given to the repression tendency when it operates in therapy. On a behavioral level, resistance refers to certain kinds of observable actions of the patient in therapy. On a conceptual level, resistance was conceived as a psychological force, a countercharge, in the patient that opposed the therapist's efforts to get him to remember in the early days of psychoanalysis and to cure him in the broadest later formulations. This counterforce is observable outside of therapy as well as in. The general name for all its manifestations became "anticathexis." "Resistance" is the special name for the anticathectic force as it appears specifically in the therapeutic situation.

Resistance is unconscious, the patient being unaware of his opposition to the therapist's efforts to change him. It varies in strength with different phases of therapy; it is particularly strong when a new topic is begun and during the period immediately preceding an interpretation by the analyst.

The concept of resistance grew with the psychoanalytic theory as a whole. By 1926 Freud was distinguishing at least five types of resistance. The first three of these were resistances that came from the ego's opposition to the analyst's efforts.

1. Repression-resistance. When the concept of resistance grew beyond its early bounds, Freud gave the name "repression-resistance" to all the types of resistance that he had first distinguished. Repression-resistance centers around the patient's attempts to evade the rule in therapy that he must tell everything that comes to his mind, but broadly includes almost any action by the patient that delays or obstructs therapy. Freud specifically indicated at least thirteen kinds of behavior that he considered to be indicators of repression-resistance: (1) Making mental reservations to exempt certain information from the rule to tell everything. (2) Associative blocks as manifested by silence and inability to think of anything to say. (3) Giving absurd associations. (4) Systematically avoiding certain topics in free association. (5) Expressing an intellectual opposition to the theory of psychoanalysis on scientific grounds. (6) Developing a theoretical interest in psychoanalysis and wanting to be instructed in the theory by the therapist and to spend time in therapy discussing the theory and literature. (7) Concealing reservations about the validity of psychoanalysis as a therapeutic procedure. (8) Seizing upon various accidental occurrences as excuses to interrupt, delay, or obstruct therapy. (9) Expressing doubt about the correctness of remembered details of past events or of dreams. (10) Changing the details of dreams upon second telling. (11) Forgetting details of dreams and of past events. (12) Repeating certain themes in a monotonous and rigid way. (13) Feelings of unpleasure experienced by the patient in undertaking and carrying out the work of therapy.

2. Transference-resistance. When all the patient's repression-resistances have been interpreted by the analyst, the patient can no longer use these

ways of trying to protect himself against the analyst's efforts to change him. At this point, Freud said, the patient has recourse to transference-resistance, the most powerful resistance of all. Transference refers to the development of certain kinds of feelings toward the therapist. Transference feelings exist from the outset of treatment, but these at first take the form of an affectionate interest in the therapist that Freud names "positive transference." Positive transference is not a form of resistance. After repression resistances have been interpreted away, the normal positive transference begins to be distorted as a further means of resistance. Transference becomes resistance when a hostile or "negative transference" replaces the normal positive relationship; or when affection is turned into a manifest sexual love interest in the therapist as a means of avoiding the painful work of therapy.

There are two explanations of how transference can function as a resistance. According to the first, the transference relationship is based upon childhood sexual motives regressively activated. The psychological forces that caused the regression now appear in the form of transference-resistances. According to the second, the unconscious processes exercise an attraction (on the analogy of a magnet) upon these regressively aroused childhood motives and function as a force that pulls them in the direction of remaining as a part of the unconscious.

Fundamentally, Freud regarded the development of transference-resistance as a protective substitute for remembering the significant events of childhood. In the absence of such a defensive need, Freud believed that this remembering would naturally occur and, in that case, transference-resistance would not develop.

3. Resistance from the gain of illness. The patient's illness brings him certain secondary advantages, just as a soldier's pension works as a reward for his injuries, and because the patient is reluctant to give up these gains, he fights against getting well.

4. Resistance from a sense of guilt. This form of resistance is based upon a need to suffer. The person's over-strong superego demands that he should be punished and he prefers to remain sick to satisfy these needs for self-punishment originating in the superego.

5. Resistance of the unconscious. This is also based upon a need to suffer, and has its origins in certain tendencies of the id. There is the repetition-compulsion tendency. Psychic processes have an innate tendency to reinstate earlier existing conditions. Unconscious processes are particu-

larly subject to such tendencies to repeat. In therapy this results in the same tendencies coming up over and over and necessitates a period of "working through" during which already interpreted themes reappear regularly in manifestly new guises each of which has to be patiently interpreted anew. Unconscious processes also tend to act like magnetic forces in that they draw to themselves conscious processes that relate to what is already in the unconscious. The id, as the repository of unconscious material, works to draw normally conscious material that is related to it into the id, and to keep part of it from being made conscious by the analyst's interpretations.

Freud also attributed resistance of the unconscious to a loss of psychic plasticity on the part of the patient, "an exhaustion of the capacity for change and development," and compared it with the rigidity normally found only in very old people.

Resistance of the unconscious differs from the other forms of resistance in that no independent behavioral correlates were definitely specified by Freud. The patient simply fails to improve and resistance of the unconscious (or of the id) is in the nature of a hypothesis to explain such failure in cases not explained by the other four forms of resistance.

V

⌁ Successful Defenses

T<small>HUS</small> far we have dealt with four different manifestations of the forces of repression and defense:

1. Repressive defenses (including amnesic repression, which can be regarded separately for some purposes).
2. Regression as a "nonrepressive" defense.
3. Inhibitory defenses.
4. Resistances.

These types of defense are all "unsuccessful" in the sense that they do not accomplish their aim of eliminating the dangerous impulses. Since the anxiety-causing instinctual forces are only disguised or inhibited, or are replaced with other anxiety-linked impulses, the person's fundamental problem remains unsolved. The "successful defenses" to be dealt with in this chapter have a radically different outcome in that the objectionable impulse is done away with.

The terms "successful defense" and "unsuccessful defense" do not represent any consistent usage on Freud's part. But it is appropriate to adopt them since Freud did use both terms at least casually in his writing and, further, there is no doubt that he made an underlying conceptual distinction of this kind even though he did not give it a name. The existence of such a distinction is clearest in Freud's later writings, as will become evident in the quotations used in the various sections of this chapter. This probably is the reason for the neglect of the distinction in Freudian literature. The public image of Freudian theory seems to be firmly based on the writings of the 1900 to 1915 period, and the professional image, too, has tended not to take full account of changes and developments that occurred later.

Most of Freud's writings are about the unsuccessful defenses seen in the clinic. In fact, he used "repression" and "defense" almost exclusively to refer to those cases in which the ego-protective effort did not succeed. But as his theory matured Freud became increasingly concerned with constructing a general psychology of the human mind; and while giving attention to man in everyday life as well as in the clinic, he developed ideas on how normal persons handle the threats of anxiety that cripple the clinic patient. Freud's psychology of normal or successful defense is fragmentary in the extreme as compared to the voluminous accounts of the clinical concepts. In some cases it is not even certain whether Freud was using a casual phrase or referring to a seriously meant concept. In others it is not clear whether different names are alternate terms for the same idea or whether two concepts are involved. Nevertheless these efforts to encompass normalcy were real and represent an important turn in Freud's thinking on repression and defense.

"SUCCESSFUL REPRESSION" AND "SUCCESSFUL DEFENSE"

It is worth examining, first, some instances of Freud's use of the terms "successful" and "unsuccessful" in referring to both repression and defense.

Here are two typical quotations from the middle and late periods of Freud's writings in which successful repression is referred to:

"If a repression does not succeed in preventing feelings of unpleasure or anxiety from arising, we may say that it has failed, even though it may have achieved its purpose as far as the ideational portion is concerned. Repressions that have failed will of course have more claim on our interest than any that may have been successful; for the latter will for the most part escape our examination." (1915b, p. 153.)

"A symptom arises from an instinctual impulse which has been detrimentally affected by repression. If the ego, by making use of the signal of unpleasure, attains its object of completely suppressing the instinctual impulse, we learn nothing of how this has happened. We can only find out about it from those cases in which repression must be described as having to a greater or less extent failed." (1926a, pp. 94–95.)

The 1936 translation of Freud's *Inhibitions, Symptoms and Anxiety* by Henry A. Bunker phrased the last sentence of the second quotation as "We learn something about it only from the cases in which repression is more or less unsuccessful" (1926b, pp. 21–22).

73

In these comments, Freud reveals that successful repression is a process that cannot be studied by the usual procedures of psychoanalysis. In unsuccessful repression the patient is left with a strong motive that is distorted, misrepresented, or inhibited, and this motive has effects upon the person's behavior in therapy, effects from which the presence and character of the disguised or inhibited motive can be inferred. In successful repression or successful defense, the dangerous motive ceases to exist and cannot be studied in therapy because it does not affect behavior. This is the reason Freud says, in the above quotations, that successful repressions "will for the most part escape our examination," and "If the ego . . . attains its object of completely suppressing the instinctual impulse, we learn nothing of how this has happened."

Since Freud used the term "defense" relatively little after the early years, it is hard to find late passages in which he spoke of successful defense in the same sense that he did of successful repression. Here is a passage from the early period when he used "defense" and "repression" as synonyms:

"In the first period [Freud is speaking of the development of obsessional neurosis], that of childish immorality, occur the experiences containing the germ of the neurosis which develops later; first of all in very early childhood the experiences of sexual seduction that make subsequent repression possible, then the deeds of sexual aggression against the opposite sex which appear later as acts to which self-reproach becomes attached.

"This period is brought to a close by the onset of sexual 'maturity', often itself premature. No self-reproach becomes connected with the memories of those pleasurable activities, and the relation with the initial passive experience makes it possible to repress them and substitute for them a *primary defence-symptom* — often only after conscious and remembered efforts. Conscientiousness, shame and self-distrust are the kind of symptoms which introduce the third period, that of apparent health, or better, that of *successful defence*.

"The next period, that of illness, is distinguished by the *return of the repressed memories*, i.e. by failure of the defence . . ." (1896, pp. 162–63.)

In this case Freud was using "successful" to refer to a period of stability. This was a temporary state, however. Since the repressed primal impulses later returned, they presumably were not actually abolished during the period of "successful defense." This would seem to be different from the outcome in some of the other types of successful defenses to be described in this chapter. Freud's conceptual meaning in this case would be more accurately stated by a term such as "stable repression" or "stable defense" — hence a period during which the repressed impulse is quiescent but not actually abolished, retaining the potential of "returning" under altered conditions. One important but probably unresolvable problem is whether, in other types of successful defense (such as "destruction in the id," or "judgmental repudiation"), the same kind of latent potential for "return of the repressed" also exists, or whether such a potential has been permanently abolished.

"DESTRUCTION IN THE ID"

One of Freud's few definite statements on successful defense is contained in his account of how normal persons deal with the impulses of the Oedipus complex. He sharply contrasts the unsuccessful solutions of pathology with "destruction of the impulse in id" in normalcy:

"The object-cathexes are given up [in the normal solution of the Oedipus complex] and replaced by identification. The authority of the father or the parents is introjected into the ego and there forms the kernel of the super-ego, which takes its severity from the father, perpetuates his prohibition against incest, and so insures the ego against a recurrence of the libidinal object-cathexis. The libidinal trends belonging to the Oedipus-complex are in part desexualized and sublimated, which probably happens with every transformation into identification; in part they are inhibited in their aim and changed into affectionate feelings. The whole process, on the one hand, preserves the genital organ, wards off the danger of losing it; on the other hand, it paralyzes it, takes away its function from it. This process introduces the latency period which now interrupts the child's sexual development.

"I see no reason to deny the name of 'repression' to the ego's turning from the Oedipus-complex, although later repressions are for the most part effected with the participation of the super-ego, which is only built up during this process. But the process described is more than a repression; when carried out in the ideal way it is equivalent to destruction and abrogation of the complex. It is not a great step to assume that here we have come upon the borderland between normal and pathological which is never very sharply defined. If the ego has really not achieved much more than a repression of the complex, then this latter persists uncon-

sciously in the *id*, and will express itself later on in some pathogenic effect."
(1924, p. 273.)

In this statement, Freud calls this process "repression," but, on the other hand, clearly states that it is "more than a repression" in that it achieves a destruction of the impulse rather than mere exclusion from awareness and motility. This distinction was repeated even more clearly in 1933: "Now let us go back to a consideration of the id. It is not so easy to discover what it is that happens during the progress of repression to the impulses that are being opposed. The main question to which we want to know the answer is: What happens to the energy, to the libidinal charge of the impulse, and how is it used? . . . We are therefore prepared to believe that the effects of repression will be very varied, and sometimes more and sometimes less extensive. In many cases the repressed impulse may retain its libidinal cathexis, and continue to exist unaltered in the id, although under the perpetual pressure of the ego ['unsuccessful defense']. In other instances it seems to undergo complete destruction, in which case its libido is finally diverted into other channels ['successful defense']. I have suggested that this is what happens where the Oedipus complex is dealt with normally. In this desirable state of affairs, the Oedipus complex would thus not merely be repressed, but would be actually destroyed in the id." (1933, pp. 126–27.)

These statements establish clearly that normal people use a different means of handling Oedipus impulses than do neurotics. "Destruction" here can scarcely mean anything but the total abolition of the impulse.

While the conceptual distinction between destruction in the id and repression is plainly made, Freud seems reluctant in the foregoing quotations to attach a new term to the concept, saying (in the first quotation) that he sees no reason to deny the name "repression" to the process! It is small wonder that confusion exists about the meaning of "repression."

Freud's statements on destruction in the id are his clearest pronouncements on the difference between successful and unsuccessful defense. These quotations say unequivocally that in unsuccessful defense, the dangerous impulse is *not* abolished; it is merely disguised (or inhibited) and will persist unconsciously and express itself in behavior. In successful defense there is no continuation of the undesirable impulse after the defensive process has taken place; the impulse, in its original form at least, disappears. Hence, in successful defense one cannot expect to find any sort of evidence for the existence of the dangerous impulse in behavior.

There are no "derivatives," no continuing but hidden and unconscious influences. The only evidence for successful defense would be an early history showing the presence of the impulse in question and a later one showing its absence.

SUBLIMATION

The best known and the earliest distinguished form of successful defense is, of course, sublimation. Freud first wrote of it in the *Three Essays on the Theory of Sexuality* of 1905. The first of the two passages from that work pertaining to sublimation is from a section entitled "Reaction-Formation and Sublimation":

"What is it that goes to the making of these constructions which are so important for the growth of a civilized and normal individual? They probably emerge at the cost of the infantile sexual impulses themselves. Thus the activity of those impulses does not cease even during this period of latency, though their sexual energy is diverted, wholly or in great part, from their sexual use and directed to other ends. Historians of civilization appear to be at one in assuming that powerful components are acquired for every kind of cultural achievement by this diversion of sexual instinctual forces from sexual aims and their directions to new ones — a process which deserves the name of 'sublimation'. To this we would add, accordingly, that the same process plays a part in the development of the individual and we would place its beginning in the period of sexual latency of childhood.

"It is possible further to form some idea of the mechanism of this process of sublimation. On the one hand, it would seem, the sexual impulses cannot be utilized during these years of childhood, since the reproductive functions have been deferred — a fact which constitutes the main feature of the period of latency. On the other hand, these impulses would seem in themselves to be perverse — that is, to arise from erotogenic zones and to derive their activity from instincts which, in view of the direction of the subject's development, can only arouse unpleasurable feelings. They consequently evoke opposing mental forces (reacting impulses) which, in order to suppress this unpleasure effectively, build up the mental dams that I have already mentioned — disgust, shame, and morality." (1905a, p. 178.)

In 1915 Freud added this footnote to the section: "In the case which I am here discussing, the sublimation of sexual instinctual forces takes place along the path of reaction-formation. But in general, it is possible to distinguish the concepts of sublimation and reaction-formation from each other as two different processes. Sublimation can also take place by other and simpler mechanisms." (1905a, pp. 178–79.)

At the end of the *Three Essays* Freud wrote a summary, one section of which was entitled "Sublimation": "The third alternative result of an abnormal constitutional disposition is made possible by the process of sublimation. This enables excessively strong excitations arising from particular sources of sexuality to find an outlet and use in other fields, so that a not inconsiderable increase in psychical efficiency results from a disposition which in itself is perilous. Here we have one of the origins of artistic activity; and, according to the completeness or incompleteness of the sublimation, a characterological analysis of a highly gifted individual, and in particular of one with an artistic disposition, may reveal a mixture, in every proportion, of efficiency, perversion and neurosis. A sub-species of sublimation is to be found in suppression by reaction-formation, which, as we have seen, begins during a child's period of latency and continues in favourable cases throughout his whole life. What we describe as a person's 'character' is built up to a considerable extent from the material of sexual excitations and is composed of instincts that have been fixed since childhood, of constructions achieved by means of sublimation, and of other constructions, employed for effectively holding in check perverse impulses which have been recognized as being unutilizable. The multifariously perverse sexual disposition of childhood can accordingly be regarded as the source of a number of our virtues, in so far as through reaction-formation it stimulates their development." (1905a, pp. 238–39.)

These quotations establish several points:

1. Sublimation is used in normal development as a means of dealing with sexual impulses.

2. In sublimation a sexual motive is replaced by a social, culturally approved one.

3. Sublimation begins to be used as a defense at the beginning of the latency period.

4. The sexual impulses involved are pregenital and, in 1905, were apparently conceived of as being particularly strong. Apparently Freud thought, at that time, that only strong pregenital impulses had to be sublimated.

5. Sublimation is contrasted with repression. This is not explicitly

evident in the quotations, but the second of these lists sublimation as the "third alternative" in the situation — continuance of pregenital sex as perversion being the first alternative, repression the second.

6. In 1905, Freud conceived the mechanism of sublimation as being reaction-formation. He did not later repeat this statement, according to Harry B. Levy's conclusion from his extensive study of the sublimation concept (14).

7. Artistic activity is an example of sublimation.

A good general account of sublimation is given by Freud in his *General Introduction to Psychoanalysis*: "In general, there are very many ways by which it is possible to endure lack of libidinal satisfaction without falling ill. Above all we know of people who are able to take such abstinence upon themselves without injury; they are then not happy, they suffer from unsatisfied longing, but they do not become ill. We therefore have to conclude that the sexual impulse-excitations are exceptionally 'plastic,' if I may use the word. One of them can step in place of another; if satisfaction of one is desired in reality, satisfaction of another can offer full recompense. They are related to one another like a network of communicating canals filled with fluid, and this in spite of their subordination to the genital primacy, a condition which is not at all easily reduced to an image. Further the component-instincts of sexuality, as well as the united sexual impulse which comprises them, show a great capacity to change their object, to exchange it for another — i.e. for one more easily attainable; this capacity for displacement and readiness to accept surrogates must produce a powerful counter-effect to the effect of a frustration. One amongst these processes serving as protection against illness arising from want has reached a particular significance in the development of culture. It consists in the abandonment, on the part of the sexual impulse, of an aim previously found either in the gratification of a component-impulse or in the gratification incidental to reproduction, and the adoption of a new aim — which new aim, though genetically related to the first, can no longer be regarded as sexual, but must be called social in character. We call this process SUBLIMATION, by which we subscribe to the general standard which estimates social aims above sexual (ultimately selfish) aims. Incidentally, sublimation is merely a special case of the connections existing between sexual impulses and other, asexual ones." (1916–17, p. 302.)

Freud was definite that sublimation did not involve repression: "As we have learnt, the formation of an ideal heightens the demands of the ego and is the most powerful factor favouring repression; sublimation is a way out, a way by which those demands can be met *without* involving repression" (1914b, p. 95).

The last two quotations make it clear that in sublimation ego-protection is achieved by the substitution of one drive for another, a social motive replacing a sexual one; the dangerous impulse (sexual) is dealt with in a way that is not repressive, and hence it must be altered rather than merely distorted, inhibited, or replaced by an equally dangerous regressive impulse.

Freud regarded sublimation as a mechanism that could only deal with limited amounts of sex motivation. In addition, its use seemed to be restricted to a few people: "The plasticity and free mobility of the libido is not by any means retained to the full in all of us; and sublimation can never discharge more than a certain proportion of libido, apart from the fact that many people possess the capacity for sublimation only in a slight degree . . ." (1916–17, p. 303).

Freud's distinction between sublimation and the formation of the ego-ideal is of some help in establishing a clear picture of sublimation: "We are naturally led to examine the relation between this forming of an ideal and sublimation. Sublimation is a process that concerns object-libido and consists in the instinct's directing itself towards an aim other than, and remote from, that of sexual satisfaction; in this process the accent falls upon deflection from sexuality. Idealization is a process that concerns the *object*; by it that object, without any alteration in its nature, is aggrandized and exalted in the subject's mind. . . . In so far as sublimation describes something that has to do with the instinct and idealization something to do with the object, the two concepts are to be distinguished from each other." (1914b, p. 94.)

The following quotations from *The Ego and the Id* illustrate the trend of Freud's later writings on sublimation. Among other things, they suggest that Freud came to see "desexualization" as being involved in sublimation:

"The transformation of object-libido into narcissistic libido which thus takes place obviously implies an abandonment of sexual aims, a process of desexualization; it is consequently a kind of sublimation. Indeed, the question arises, and deserves careful consideration, whether this is not always the path taken in sublimation, whether all sublimation does not take place through the agency of the ego, which begins by changing sexual

80

object-libido into narcissistic libido and then, perhaps, goes on to give it another aim." (1923, pp. 37–38.)

"It appears, however, that . . . we have tacitly made another assumption which deserves to be formulated explicitly. We have reckoned as though there existed in the mind — whether in the ego or the id — a displaceable energy, which is in itself neutral, but is able to join forces either with an erotic or with a destructive impulse." (1923, pp. 61–62.)

"It seems a plausible view that this neutral displaceable energy, which is probably active alike in the ego and in the id, proceeds from the narcissistic reservoir of libido, *i.e.* that it is desexualized Eros" (1923, pp. 62–63).

"If this displaceable energy is desexualized libido, it might also be described as sublimated energy; for it would still retain the main purpose of Eros — that of uniting and binding — in so far as it helped towards establishing that unity, or tendency to unity, which is particularly characteristic of the ego. If the intellectual processes in the wider sense are to be classed among these displacements, then the energy for the work of thought itself must be supplied from sublimated erotic sources." (1923, p. 64.)

"The super-ego arises, as we know, from an identification with the father regarded as a model. Every such identification is in the nature of a desexualization or even of a sublimation." (1923, p. 80.)

These quotations leave unclear the exact relationship between desexualization and sublimation. A later passage from 1924, which is reproduced in full on pages 75–76 above, suggests that the two concepts are not one, since Freud uses the phrase "desexualized and sublimated." Some of the preceding quotations also suggest two processes, or at least indicate that desexualization and sublimation are not identical. Most passages suggest that the process of desexualization is a part of sublimation, but that sublimation involves more than desexualization. Desexualization involves a removal of sexual elements from a motive; sublimation involves not only this, but also an active replacement with another, socially acceptable motive. The difference between the two comes out most clearly in the concept of "desexualized libido." This desexualized energy is "neutral," Freud says, which implies that it has no motivational direction of its own. A sublimated impulse, such as scientific curiosity replacing childhood scoptophilia, is not such a neutral energy since it has a definite direction in its orientation to science.

Harry B. Levy's extensive study of sublimation (14) should be consulted by anyone interested in the concept. He makes the following points about Freud's theory of sublimation: After introducing the concept in *Three Essays on the Theory of Sexuality* in 1905, Freud's writing about sublimation showed very little change over the years. In 1905 Freud considered pregenital sex to be the main source of sublimated energy and seemed to think that reaction-formation was the mechanism of sublimation. In that work and throughout his writings Freud used artistic production as his main example of sublimation. In later writings Freud did not again mention reaction-formation as a mechanism of sublimation but described it as a displacement of sexual energy.

REPUDIATION OR CONDEMNATION

One successful means of dealing with anxiety-linked impulses of an objectionable nature was distinguished by Freud as "condemnation" based on judgment: "At some later period, rejection based on judgment (*condemnation*) will be found to be a good method to adopt against an instinctual impulse. Repression is a preliminary stage of condemnation, something between flight and condemnation." (1915b, p. 146.)

Freud's distinction between condemnation or repudiation and repression is given in the following passage from *A General Introduction to Psychoanalysis*: "It will now be necessary to make our conception of this process of *repression* more precise . . . Let us take as a model an impulse, a mental process seeking to convert itself into action: we know that it can suffer rejection, by virtue of what we call 'repudiation' or 'condemnation'; whereupon the energy at its disposal is withdrawn, it becomes powerless, but it can continue to exist as a memory. The whole process of decision on the point takes place with the full cognizance of the ego. It is very different when we imagine the same impulse subject to *repression*; it would then retain its energy and no memory of it would be left behind; the process of repression, too, would be accomplished without the cognizance of the ego." (1916–17, p. 259.)

Presumably Freud was referring to repudiation when he distinguished repression from the "assimilation of the impulse to the ego" in the *New Introductory Lectures*: "Our next question will be: How can we picture the process of repression carried out under the influence of anxiety? I think this is what happens: the ego becomes aware that the satisfaction of some nascent instinctual demand would evoke one among the well-remembered danger-situations. This instinctual cathexis must, therefore, somehow or

82

other be suppressed, removed, made powerless. We know that the ego succeeds in this task if it is strong, and if it has assimilated the impulse in question into its organization [by its becoming conscious and condemned?]. In the case of repression, however, the impulse is still part of the id, and the ego feels weak. In such a contingency, the ego calls to its aid a technique, which is, at bottom, identical with that of normal thinking. Thinking is an experimental dealing with small quantities of energy, just as a general moves miniature figures about over a map before setting his troops in motion. In this way, the ego anticipates the satisfaction of the questionable impulse, and enables it to reproduce the painful feelings which are attached to the beginning of the dreaded danger-situation. Thereupon the automatic mechanism of the pleasure-pain principle is brought into play and carries through the repression of the dangerous impulse." (1933, p. 124.)

Freud's clearest statement on judgmental repudiation occurs in "A Disturbance of Memory on the Acropolis": "There are an extraordinarily large number of methods (or mechanisms, as we say) used by our ego in the discharge of its defensive functions . . . The most primitive and thoroughgoing of these methods, 'repression', was the starting-point of the whole of our deeper understanding of psycho-pathology. Between repression and what may be termed the normal method of warding off what is painful or unbearable, by means of recognizing it, considering it, making a judgment upon it and taking appropriate action about it, there lie a whole series of more or less clearly pathological methods of behaviour on the part of the ego." (1936, pp. 309–10.)

Judgmental repudiation or condemnation appears to be the main mechanism of cure in therapy. Once the analyst makes his interpretations and the dangerous impulse becomes conscious, cure follows if the person can condemn or repudiate the impulse and thus dispose of it for good and all. It is an interesting fact that this rational intellectual mechanism is, in a theory of psychology that is widely considered to be a psychology of unreason, the ultimate means by which man's irrationality is overcome.

THE ABSORPTION OF INSTINCTS

In *Civilization and Its Discontents* Freud discussed the modifications that culture brings about in human instincts and suggested that there are three general changes: the instincts may become (1) "absorbed," (2) sublimated, or (3) suppressed or repressed (1930, pp. 61–63). His statement is of interest in that he definitely distinguishes "absorption" of instinct from sublimation and repression as an outcome. His account of absorption is as follows: "The evolution of culture seems to us a peculiar kind of process passing over humanity, of which several aspects strike us as familiar. We can describe this process in terms of the modifications it effects on the known human instinctual dispositions, which it is the economic task of our lives to satisfy. Some of these instincts become absorbed, as it were, so that something appears in place of them which in an individual we call a character-trait. The most remarkable example of this process is found in respect of the anal erotism of young human beings. Their primary interest in the excretory function, its organs and products, is changed in the course of their growth into a group of traits that we know well — thriftiness, orderliness, and cleanliness . . ." (1930, pp. 61–62.)

Absorption of instinct would then seem to be the mechanism for character formation, a mechanism separate from sublimation and repression-suppression, though its relation to other successful defenses is not clear.

"Absorption" is applied in the quotation above to a change that Freud would earlier have attributed to reaction-formation. It is possible that the concept of absorption explains what happened to Freud's first conception of sublimation as employing the mechanism of reaction-formation. Perhaps absorption is a mechanism of sublimation along with desexualization, and all three differ from reaction-formation.

SUCCESSFUL AND UNSUCCESSFUL DEFENSE IN NORMAL PERSONS

It is clear from the evidence of this chapter that Freud distinguished some successful ways of dealing with impulses, and considered that these characterized normalcy as opposed to pathology. Further, he made many statements such as the following to the effect that repression is a pathological mechanism:

"The pathogenic process which is demonstrated by the resistances we call REPRESSION" (1916–17, p. 259).

"If we survey the whole situation we arrive at a simple formula for the origins of a neurosis: the ego has made at attempt to suppress certain portions of the id *in an inappropriate manner*, this attempt has failed and the id has taken its revenge. A neurosis is thus the result of a conflict between the ego and the id, upon which the ego has embarked because, as careful investigation shows, it wishes at all costs to retain its adaptability in relation to the real external world. The disagreement is between the external world and the id; and it is because the ego, loyal to its inmost nature, takes sides with the external world that it becomes involved in conflict with its id. But please observe that what creates the determinant for the illness is not the fact of this conflict — for disagreements of this kind between reality and the id are unavoidable and it is one of the ego's standing tasks to mediate in them — but the circumstance that the ego has made use of the inefficient instrument of repression for dealing with the conflict. But this in turn is due to the fact that the ego, at the time at which it was set the task, was undeveloped and powerless. The decisive repressions all take place in early childhood." (1926a, pp. 203–4.)

Thus far we seem to have a clear division. On the one hand there are neurotics, who use the pathological response of unsuccessful repression or defense; and on the other hand, we have normal persons, who use the successful defense mechanisms outlined in this chapter. But the picture is not that sharply outlined. Freud also made statements to the effect that normal persons use *repressive* ways (unsuccessful defenses) of handling impulses. Referring to his *Three Essays on the Theory of Sexuality* of 1905, he said: "I showed that *normality* is a result of the repression of certain component instincts and constituents of the infantile disposition and of the subordination of the remaining constituents under the primacy of the genital zones in the service of the reproductive function" (1906, p. 277).

Of course a question might arise here as to whether, in this case, Freud was being loose with his terminology and wrote "repression" where, strictly speaking, he ought to have written "sublimation." As we saw, he was not averse to calling destruction in the id "repression" in the same paper in which he sharply distinguished it from what is here called "unsuccessful repression." That is possible, but there are other instances when he was discussing the psychology of normal persons in which Freud seems to have used "repression" to mean "unsuccessful repression." Thus, as Brenner points out, Freud clearly included normal persons as repressors in his books on *Wit and Its Relation to the Unconscious* and the *Psychopathology of Everyday Life* (4, pp. 24–25).

Is Freud being contradictory here? If so, the following quotation seems to resolve the apparent inconsistency:

"The dreams of neurotics, however, differ in no essential from those of normal people; they are indeed perhaps not in any way distinguishable from them . . . We have to conclude therefore that the difference be-

85

tween neurosis and health prevails only by day; it is not sustained in dream-life. It thus becomes necessary to transfer to healthy persons a number of conclusions arrived at as a result of the connections between the dreams and the symptoms of neurotics. We have to recognize that the healthy man as well possesses those factors in mental life which alone can bring about the formation of a dream or of a symptom, and we must conclude further that the healthy also have instituted repressions and have to expend a certain amount of energy to maintain them; that their unconscious minds too harbour repressed impulses which are still suffused with energy, and that a *part of the libido is in them also withdrawn from the disposal of the ego*. The healthy man too is virtually a neurotic, but the only symptom that he *seems* capable of developing is a dream. To be sure when you subject his waking life also to a critical investigation you discover something that contradicts this specious conclusion; for this apparently healthy life is pervaded by innumerable trivial and practically unimportant symptom-formations.

"The difference between nervous health and nervous illness (neurosis) is narrowed down therefore to a practical distinction, and is determined by the practical result — how far the person concerned remains capable of a sufficient degree of capacity for enjoyment and active achievement in life. The difference can probably be traced back to the proportion of the energy which has remained free relative to that of the energy which has been bound by repression, i.e. it is a quantitative and not a qualitative difference." (1916–17, pp. 397–98.)

Here Freud seems to say clearly that normal people use the unsuccessful defenses that neurotics employ. Apparently it is a matter of degree. Normal persons use *both* successful and unsuccessful defenses. Presumably they mainly use successful defenses, but Freud does not really say what the balance between the two types of response is in normal cases. At least it is definite that it is a relative matter.

SUMMARY

Successful defenses are those in which ego-protection is achieved by making an actual change in the dangerous impulse itself rather than merely disguising or inhibiting it as in unsuccessful defense. Successful defenses are not only "impulse-altering" defenses; the alteration must be in an acceptable direction.

The concept of successful defense was introduced by Freud as early

SUCCESSFUL DEFENSES

as 1905 in his account of sublimation in the *Three Essays on the Theory of Sexuality*, but the idea was not developed until the last period of his writing. Even in these final works the concept is a fragmentary one and represents an unfinished theoretical turn in Freud's attempts to extend his psychology to cover normal personality development. Virtually all of Freud's writings on repression and defense are about the unsuccessful kind.

The terms "successful" and "unsuccessful" are suggested herein both because Freud sometimes used these terms — if casually — in the senses meant here, and because there is no doubt that a distinction between the two did exist in Freud's thinking even though he did not give it a separate name that he used in any consistent way.

In speaking of what are here called "successful defenses" Freud sometimes, and once very clearly, described them as forms of repression. Usually he distinguished them sharply from repression.

"Destruction in the id" is Freud's clearest example of a successful defense and one which he described repeatedly in his later writings. This is the mechanism used by normal persons to deal with the Oedipus complex. When successfully carried out, Freud said, ". . . the Oedipus complex would thus not merely be repressed, but would actually be destroyed in the id." Freud did not name this defense; he called it a form of repression even though, as in the line quoted, he sharply distinguished it from repression in its usual meaning of unsuccessful defense.

Destruction in the id shows best the essential point that in successful defense the dangerous impulse is actually altered in such a way as to change its unacceptable character. In unsuccessful defense, the impulse is usually disguised by some alteration of consciousness, or it is inhibited. In regression it may also be altered, but the alteration is not one that changes its unacceptable character. Actual change of impulse from unacceptable to acceptable (including "destruction") is thus the essential distinguishing feature of successful defense.

Sublimation was the form of successful defense first distinguished by Freud. Although first described in 1905, the concept received very little theoretical attention. Sublimation shows the following features:

1. The impulses that are sublimated are pregenital, being principally oral and anal in character.

2. The pregenital impulse is replaced by a social, culturally approved motive.

87

3. Sublimation begins to be used as a defense at the beginning of the latency period.

4. The mechanism of sublimation was at first conceived as being reaction-formation, but since this conception never reappeared in Freud's later writings, it may represent a point on which he changed his mind without ever saying so. In his later writings, Freud said that "desexualization" was involved in sublimation without making clear the relationship of the two. It is probable that desexualization is the more limited concept, referring simply to the removal of sexual elements from a motive which thus changes it into a "neutral" form of energy, whereas sublimation involves not only this as a first step, but also the active replacement of the desexualized motive with a socially acceptable one. A sublimation cannot be merely "neutral"; a desexualized motive can be.

5. Freud regarded sublimation as a mechanism that could deal only with limited amounts of sexual motivation and considered that many persons possessed only a slight capacity for sublimation.

6. Freud used artistic activity as virtually his only specific example of sublimation in all his writings on the topic, although he seemed to imply that most of man's cultural achievements come from his use of this mechanism.

Repudiation or condemnation is the successful means of dealing with unacceptable impulses made conscious by the analyst's interpretations in therapy. In this response the impulse is rejected on the basis of judgment. Freud explicitly contrasted this handling of the impulse with repression. Apparently repudiation is a means of dealing with dangerous impulses generally as well as in therapy. Repudiation leaves the person with a conscious memory of the impulse but destroys its motivational power.

Absorption was explicitly distinguished from both sublimation and repression by Freud. As an example of absorption he used the replacement of anal motives in childhood by such traits as thriftiness, orderliness, and cleanliness — which, earlier, he would have called reaction-formation. The relation of absorption to other successful defenses is unclear.

Normal persons use both successful and unsuccessful defenses. Apparently the difference between normalcy and pathology lies in the extent to which one or the other type of defense is used.

VI

✕. Primal Repression

ONE of the most intriguing, important, and least discussed aspects of Freud's theory of repression and defense is his idea that adult repression is dependent upon the prior existence of childhood repressions. Without a history of such "primal repressions," to use the term Freud adopted, an adult would not be able to use repression (called "repression proper," or "after-expulsion," or "after-pressure" when Freud was distinguishing it from early repressions) as a means of ego-protection. This was a point that Freud made very early in his writings and insisted upon throughout in the strongest terms. The neglect of this whole topic in our psychology textbook accounts of Freud can only be ascribed to the difficulty of piecing together the complete theory.

The importance of the concept in psychoanalysis is very great. Primal repression is regarded as the main mechanism by which childhood influences become so persistent in later life, by which "the child is father to the man." It is thus a key to the psychoanalytic theory of mental illness.

The Freudian theory of change depends upon primal repression just as much as does the theory of persistence, since undoing childhood repressions is conceived as the main means of change. Childhood repression also is the main mechanism by which development takes place. Repression divides the ego off from the id, and, later, the superego is formed through repression of the Oedipus complex.

Primal repression, therefore, is a central concept in Freud's theory of personality. It first appeared in Freud's writings in the briefly held but historically important theory that certain neuroses were caused by seductions in childhood.

THE SEDUCTION THEORY

For several years during his early work with hysteria and obsessional neuroses, before 1900, Freud believed that he had discovered the specific causes of these two disorders in the childhood histories of his patients. They regularly reported that they had participated in seductive activities in early childhood and Freud came to conclude that such early "traumatic" experiences were the specific prerequisites for the later development of neuroses. When the supposed seductions proved to be imaginative falsifications, which Freud called "screen memories," rather than actual episodes, Freud gave up the seduction aspect of the theory, but retained the idea of childhood sexual experience as essential to later disorders. This main point of the seduction theory — that later repressive potentialities are dependent upon earlier repressed traumas — was never altered, and passages on this early theory provide the first statements of what later became the concept of primal repression:

"I cannot say for certain up to what age-limit sexual injury falls within the aetiology of hysteria; but I doubt whether sexual passivity after the eighth to tenth year can evoke repression in the absence of previous experiences of the same kind" (1896, p. 159).

"All the experiences and excitements which in the period of life after puberty prepare the way for or occasion the outbreak of hysteria can be proved to act only because they awaken the memory-trace of those traumas in childhood; this memory-trace does not become conscious but leads to a liberation of the affect and to repression" (1896, p. 159).

" 'Repression' of the memory of a painful sexual experience in maturer years is possible only for those people in whom this experience can re-activate the memory-trace of an infantile trauma" (1896, p. 160).

DEVELOPMENT OF THE CONCEPT

The essential idea behind the concept of primal repression appeared in *The Interpretation of Dreams*, which was written during the two years (1897–99) following Freud's abandonment of the theory of sex seduction.* In the course of his discussion of primary and secondary process thinking, Freud advanced the idea that infantile wishes that are contrary

---

* According to Ernest Jones, Freud gave up the theory of sex seduction late in 1897, although he did not announce this fact publicly until 1906 (1906, p. 276). (See Jones, *The Life and Work of Sigmund Freud* (New York: Basic Books, 1953), I, 265.)

to the child's later-developed morality are repressed, and these repressed infantile wishes constitute "a store of infantile memories, which . . . becomes a *sine qua non* of repression." Later adult repression depends upon the existence of such a store of repressed infantile experiences. The crucial idea is in the last paragraph, particularly the last line, of the following passage:

"When I described one of the psychical processes occurring in the mental apparatus as the 'primary' one, what I had in mind was not merely considerations of relative importance and efficiency; I intended also to choose a name which would give an indication of its chronological priority. It is true that, so far as we know, no psychical apparatus exists which possesses a primary process only and that such an apparatus is to that extent a theoretical fiction. But this much is a fact: the primary processes are present in the mental apparatus from the first, while it is only during the course of life that the secondary processes unfold, and come to inhibit and overlay the primary ones; it may even be that their complete domination is not attained until the prime of life. In consequence of the belated appearance of the secondary processes, the core of our being, consisting of unconscious wishful impulses, remains inaccessible to the understanding and inhibition of the preconscious; the part played by the latter is restricted once and for all to directing along the most expedient paths the wishful impulses that arise from the unconscious. These unconscious wishes exercise a compelling force upon all later mental trends, a force which those trends are obliged to fall in with or which they may perhaps endeavour to divert and direct to higher aims. A further result of the belated appearance of the secondary process in that a wide sphere of mnemic material is inaccessible to preconscious cathexis.

"Among these wishful impulses derived from infancy, which can neither be destroyed nor inhibited, there are some whose fulfilment would be a contradiction of the purposive ideas of secondary thinking. The fulfilment of these wishes would no longer generate an affect of pleasure but of unpleasure; and *it is precisely this transformation of affect which constitutes the essence of what we term 'repression'*. The problem of repression lies in the question of how it is and owing to what motive forces that this transformation occurs; but it is a problem that we need only touch upon here. It is enough for us to be clear that a transformation of this kind does occur in the course of development — we have only to recall the way in which disgust emerges in childhood after having been absent to begin with

91

— and that it is related to the activity of the secondary system. The memories on the basis of which the unconscious wish brings about the release of affect were never accessible to the *Pcs.*, and consequently the release of the affect attaching to those memories cannot be inhibited either. It is for the very reason of this generation of affect that these ideas are now inaccessible even by way of the preconscious thoughts on to which they have transferred their wishful force. On the contrary, the unpleasure principle takes control and causes the *Pcs.* to turn away from the transference thoughts. They are left to themselves — 'repressed' — and thus it is that the presence of a store of infantile memories, which has from the first been held back from the *Pcs.*, becomes a *sine qua non* of repression." (1900, pp. 603–4.)

By 1911 the concept of primal repression was fairly well developed, as can be seen from this passage taken from Freud's paper on the Schreber case:

"In psycho-analysis we have been accustomed to look upon pathological phenomena as being derived in a general way from repression. If we examine what is spoken of as 'repression' more closely, we shall find reason to split the process up into three phases which are easily distinguishable from one another conceptually.

"(1) The first phase consists in *fixation*, which is the precursor and necessary condition of every 'repression'. Fixation can be described in this way. One instinct or instinctual component fails to accompany the rest along the anticipated normal path of development, and, in consequence of this inhibition in its development, it is left behind at a more infantile stage. The libidinal current in question then behaves in relation to later psychological structures like one belonging to the system of the unconscious, like one that is repressed. We have already shown . . . that these instinctual fixations constitute the basis for the disposition to subsequent illness, and we may now add that they constitute above all the basis for the determination of the outcome of the third phase of repression.

"(2) The second phase of repression is that of repression proper — the phase to which most attention has hitherto been given. It emanates from the more highly developed systems of the ego — systems which are capable of being conscious — and may in fact be described as a process of 'after-pressure'. It gives an impression of being an essentially active process, while fixation appears in fact to be a passive lagging behind. What undergo repression may either be the psychical derivatives of the original lagging instincts, when these have become reinforced and so come into conflict with the ego (or ego-syntonic instincts), or they may be psychical trends which have for other reasons aroused strong aversion. But this aversion would not in itself lead to repression, unless some connection had been established between the unwelcome trends which have to be repressed and those which have been repressed already. Where this is so, the repulsion exercised by the conscious system and the attraction exercised by the unconscious one tend in the same direction towards bringing about repression. The two possibilities which are here treated separately may in practice, perhaps, be less sharply differentiated, and the distinction between them may merely depend upon the greater or lesser degree in which the primarily repressed instincts contribute to the result.

"(3) The third phase, and the most important as regards pathological phenomena, is that of failure of repression, of *irruption*, of *return of the repressed*. This irruption takes its start from the point of fixation, and it implies a regression of the libidinal development to that point.

"We have already . . . alluded to the multiplicity of the possible points of fixation; there are, in fact, as many as there are stages in the development of the libido. We must be prepared to find a similar multiplicity of the mechanisms of repression proper and of the mechanisms of irruption (or for symptom-formation), and we may already begin to suspect that it will not be possible to trace back all of these multiplicities to the developmental history of the libido alone." (1911, pp. 66–68.)

This account of Freud's makes the following points about primal repression:

1. Primal repression depends upon fixation of some components of the sexual instinct in infancy.

2. The fixated infantile impulses are unconscious, i.e., they are repressed. These fixated and repressed infantile sexual impulses constitute "primal repression." Although Freud does not use this exact term in the passages, the point is clear from later quotations to be examined.

3. Later adult repression ("repression proper," "after-pressure") would not take place except for the existence of infantile repressions (". . . this aversion would not itself lead to repression, unless some connection had been established between the unwelcome trends which have to be repressed and those which have been repressed already").

4. A neurosis involves a "return of the repressed" in which the infantile

93

repressions are reactivated ("return") when the adult attempt at repression fails.

The idea of a "return of the repressed" is an old one with Freud. It was a part of the original theory of sex seduction, where it fulfilled a corresponding role as can be seen in this account from the 1896 period, which we have already taken note of in another connection:

"In the first period [of the development of obsessional neurosis], that of childish immorality, occur the experiences containing the germ of the neurosis which develops later; first of all in very early childhood the experiences of sexual seduction that make subsequent repression possible, then the deeds of sexual aggression against the opposite sex which appear later as acts to which self-reproach becomes attached.

"This period is brought to a close by the onset of sexual 'maturity', often itself premature. No self-reproach becomes connected with the memories of those pleasurable activities, and the relation with the initial passive experience makes it possible to repress them and substitute for them a *primary defence-symptom* — often only after conscious and remembered efforts. Conscientiousness, shame and self-distrust are the kind of symptoms which introduce the third period, that of apparent health, or better, that of *successful defence*.

"The next period, that of illness, is distinguished by the *return of the repressed memories*, i.e. by failure of the defence; it is doubtful whether the awakening of these memories usually occurs accidentally or spontaneously or as a kind of by-product in consequence of current sexual disturbances. The reanimated memories and the self-reproach which is built up on them, however, never appear in consciousness unchanged. The obsessional idea and the obsessive affects which appear in consciousness and take the place of the pathogenic memory in conscious life are *compromise-formations* between the repressed and the repressing ideas." (1896, pp. 162–63.)

Freud's 1915 "Repression" paper restates, in highly condensed form, the analysis of primal repression presented in the Schreber case. In this instance he actually uses the term "primally repressed" to refer to childhood repressions:

"We have reason to assume that there is a *primal repression*, a first phase of repression, which consists in the psychical (ideational) representative of the instinct being denied entrance into the conscious. With this a *fixation* is established; the representative in question persists unaltered from then onwards and the instinct remains attached to it. This is due to the properties of unconscious processes of which we shall speak later.

"The second stage of repression, *repression proper*, affects mental derivation of the repressed representative, or such trains of thought as, originating elsewhere, have come into associative connection with it. On account of this association, these ideas experience the same fate as what was primally repressed. Repression proper, therefore, is actually an afterpressure. Moreover, it is a mistake to emphasize only the repulsion which operates from the direction of the conscious upon what is to be repressed; quite as important is the attraction exercised by what was primally repressed upon everything with which it can establish a connection. Probably the trend towards repression would fail in its purpose if these two forces did not cooperate, if there were not something previously repressed ready to receive what is repelled by the conscious." (1915b, p. 148.)

Since the foregoing represents the principal account of primal repression and its relation to adult repression that most readers of Freud have depended upon for their understanding of the theory, it should be pointed out that Freud's sketch is so condensed as to be unintelligible if taken alone. He says nothing in these passages, or in the paper itself, that identifies primal repression as *childhood* repression; nor does he note that "repression proper" is adult repression; particularly, there is no statement of their necessary interrelationship. Both his earlier and his later writings establish these points beyond doubt, but the picture has to be pieced together through study of widely scattered writings.

ANXIETY, TRAUMA, AND PRIMAL AND ADULT REPRESSION

The concept of primal repression did not achieve its final form until Freud developed the concepts of traumatic and signal anxiety in the 1926 publication *Inhibitions, Symptoms and Anxiety* and brought these ideas into relation with primal and adult repression. Up until then primal repression apparently was considered to occur simply as a phase of development; there was no clear statement from Freud as to the causal mechanism involved. Since the theory of anxiety will be presented in detail in the next chapter, a schematic summary will suffice here:

1. Anxiety in adult repression and defense acts as a warning or anticipation ("signal anxiety") of a danger.

2. The danger anticipated in adult repression and defense is that the traumas of infancy and childhood ("traumatic anxiety") will recur.

3. The infantile or childhood traumas are, fundamentally, states of overwhelming psychic helplessness.

4. The cause of such overwhelming helplessness is a state of over-tension that results when imperative infantile and childhood needs are not gratified.

5. The first and original form of such trauma is non-gratification of physiological needs (such as hunger) in infancy.

6. Later the child learns to anticipate the occurrence of such traumas. This leads to the development of various forms of such anticipatory anxiety in different periods of life: (a) Separation anxiety develops when the child learns that the infantile physiological traumas are likely to occur in the absence of the mother. (b) Castration anxiety develops at a later age because castration signifies the impossibility of union with the mother. (c) Superego anxiety develops after resolution of the Oedipus complex. Fundamentally it is this form of anxiety that is the motive for adult repression and defense. It is a signal that the earlier childhood and infantile form of trauma will recur if the adult allows his wishes to control him.

The following passages establish the relationship between signal and traumatic anxiety and primal and adult repression:

"As I have shown elsewhere, most of the repressions with which we have to deal in our therapeutic work are cases of *after*-pressure. They presuppose the operation of earlier, *primal repressions* which exert an attraction on the more recent situation. Far too little is known as yet about the background and preliminary stages of repression. There is a danger of overestimating the part played in repression by the super-ego. We cannot at present say whether it is perhaps the emergence of the super-ego which provides the line of demarcation between primal repression and after-pressure. At any rate, the earliest outbreaks of anxiety, which are of a very intense kind, occur before the super-ego has become differentiated. It is highly probable that the immediate precipitating causes of primal repressions are quantitative factors such as an excessive degree of excitation and the breaking through of the protective shield against stimuli." (1926a, p. 94.)

"Only the later repressions display the mechanism which we have described, in which anxiety is called forth as a signal of an earlier danger-situation; the earliest and most fundamental repressions arise directly from traumatic factors, where the ego comes into contact with an excessive libidinal demand; these traumatic factors create their own anxiety anew, though in accordance with the pattern of the birth-situation" (1933, p. 130).

Primal repression, then, applies to infantile and childhood traumas, presumably to all the traumas up to the development of the superego. Primal repression is a direct response to infantile trauma states due to overtension resulting from non-gratification of physiological needs in early infancy, and it is a response to the later childhood traumas that come from fears of separation from the mother and from the castration threat.

Adult repression (repression proper, after-repression, after-pressure, after-expulsion) is entirely based upon the signal-anxiety mechanism developed after the superego is formed. The adolescent or adult becomes anxious when his childhood-retained (fixated) and trauma-associated impulses threaten to become active (return of the repressed), for this would mean a recurrence of the overwhelming trauma states (helplessness) of infancy and childhood. Adult repression and defense are attempts to prevent this threatening recurrence of early traumas.

The idea of primal repression and the dependence of later adult repression upon the existence of such infantile repression was a firm principle in Freud's theory to the end, as can be seen in the following quotation from one of his last papers: "All repressions take place in early childhood; they are primitive defensive measures adopted by the immature, feeble ego. In later years there are no fresh repressions, but the old ones persist and are used by the ego for purposes of further mastering instinct. New conflicts are resolved by what we call 'after-repression.' " (1937, p. 328.)

A 1939 summary account of primal repression and repression proper (though not specifically named as such) occurs in Freud's *Moses and Monotheism*: "As a consequence of a certain experience there arises an instinctual demand which claims satisfaction. The Ego foregoes this satisfaction, either because it is paralyzed by the excessiveness of the demand [trauma] or because it recognizes in it a danger [the signal-anxiety mechanism]. The first of these reactions is the original one; both end in the avoidance of a dangerous situation. The Ego guards against this danger by repression. The excitation becomes inhibited in one way or another; the incitement, with the observations and perceptions belonging to it, is forgotten [repressed]." (1939, pp. 200–1.)

97

SUMMARY

One of Freud's earliest and most consistently held views was his belief that adult repression is only possible if the person in question already has a prior history of childhood repression. He called such early defenses "primal repression," and distinguished primal from adult repression, which he variously referred to as "repression proper," "after-expulsion," "after-repression," and "after-pressure." In terms of age, primal repression covers the period from early infancy up to a point just after the repression of the Oedipus complex.

Primal repression is a key concept in Freud's theory. It is the main mechanism that accounts for the influence of childhood experience on later life, the main means by which the ego and superego become separated from the id, and the central idea in Freudian explanations of mental illness and therapy.

The concept of primal repression first appeared in the theory of sex seduction that Freud held for a brief period between 1893 and 1897. From the fact that the histories of his first patients all showed childhood seductions, Freud postulated that such childhood experience was the specific prerequisite for the development of adult hysteria and obsessional neurosis. When he later decided that the reported seductions were childhood fantasies, he gave up the seduction aspect of the theory but continued in his succeeding ideas concerning pregenital sex to emphasize the large role of childhood sexual experience and the notion that childhood fantasy, particularly in the form of the Oedipus complex, could play a significant role in development.

In *The Interpretation of Dreams* Freud elaborated the concept of primary process thinking and attributed to infancy and childhood wishful impulses that are at first pleasurable but become unpleasurable as adult moral standards begin to affect the child. These wishful impulses are repressed, Freud said, and constitute a store of repressed infantile memories which are essential as a basis for later repression.

In formulating the theory of mental illness in 1911, Freud developed these early ideas on primal repression into a more comprehensive scheme:

1. Fixation of some components of the pregenital instincts takes place in infancy or childhood.

2. These childhood fixated impulses are repressed (primal repression).

3. Adult sex impulses are repressed (repression proper) because of

their associative connection with the repressed and fixated pregenital sex interests.

4. A neurosis develops when real-life situations concerning sex bring about a failure of adult repression. This results in a reactivation of the childhood fixations and repressions which Freud called "the return of the repressed."

The account of primal and adult repression given in the definitive "Repression" paper of 1915 followed this formulation, but was presented by Freud in such a condensed form that readers who have depended upon that essay for their picture of repression rarely appreciate that the primal repression he speaks of there is childhood repression, and that repression proper is adult repression. Freud also did not stress the necessary relationship between childhood and adult repression in the essay. Hence the 1915 account is seriously inadequate as a statement of primal repression and its role in later repression.

The concept of primal repression was not completely developed until the 1926 theory of anxiety was worked out by Freud. The following schematic outline of the new conception is necessary as a background to the final theory of primal repression:

1. The immediate motive for adult repression is anxiety. This "signal anxiety" is of an anticipatory nature, being a warning that a great danger of traumatic intensity threatens.

2. The great danger that threatens is the possibility that the traumatic states experienced in infancy and childhood are about to recur.

3. Adult repression and defense responses are reactions aimed at forestalling the recurrence of these states of traumatic anxiety once experienced in childhood.

4. The infantile and childhood traumas are, fundamentally, states of overwhelming psychic helplessness.

5. The cause of such traumatic helplessness lies in overtension resulting from non-gratification of the imperative needs of infancy and childhood. This overtension has various immediate causes at different ages: non-gratification of physiological needs in infancy; separation from the mother; and the threat of castration in later childhood.

6. With the repression of the Oedipus complex and consequent formation of the superego, the period of childhood trauma comes to an end. After that, the anxiety experienced is adult anxiety, which is an anticipation that these earlier dangers will recur.

99

The relationship of primal repression and adult repression to the theory of anxiety stated in 1926 is as follows: Primal repression refers to defensive responses to the traumas that preceded the formation of the superego. It is a primitive and automatic reaction to states of overtension deriving from non-gratification of physiological needs in infancy, and to traumas that come from experiences of separation from mother and from threat of castration in later childhood. Adult repression is based upon the signal-anxiety mechanism, which develops after the superego is formed and serves as a warning that the childhood traumas will recur if adult sexual activities that have associative connections with the childhood traumas are allowed to become active, enter consciousness, and control behavior. Adult repression and defense are attempts to prevent the recurrence of childhood trauma by protecting the ego from contemporary impulses that have such primary traumatic meanings for the person.

VII

❄️ The Motives of Repression and Defense

THE underlying structure of the theory of repression and defense is motivational: a force and counterforce working against one another. At the most abstract level, in the fully developed theory, this polarity became instincts versus anticathexis, but each side of this force and antiforce duality had a long developmental history and a complex final structure.

For purposes of exposition it is useful to use consistently the terms "force" and "counterforce" instead of Freud's various phrasings of his motivational antithesis. This constant terminology will allow the reader to keep his bearings through the many shifts of language that the ideas underwent in the development of psychoanalysis. "Force" always refers to the instinct side of the opposing motives; it strives for release, expression, discharge. "Counterforce" is the unceasing opposition to such expression that comes from the ego's need to protect itself against instincts.

FORCE AND COUNTERFORCE IN FREUD'S EARLY THEORY

The force and counterforce antithesis that had its most general expression later in instincts versus anticathexis was evident in Freud's earliest psychological writings.

In an 1893 paper Freud discussed the antithesis as seen in both normal persons and hysterics. In the former he called the force aspect "distressing antithetic ideas," which the normal person suppressed and inhibited "with the powerful self-confidence of health" ("self-confidence" corresponds to

101

"counterforce"). In persons showing hysteria, the distressing antithetic ideas are unconscious. In this case Freud called the force "counter-will," while the counterforce was the patient's "will." (1893, pp. 38–40.)

In the famous "Preliminary Communication" of 1893, written with Breuer, the force was formulated in terms of "strangulated affect" associated with memories of traumatic experiences that had not been sufficiently abreacted (1895, pp. 10 and 17). The counterforce was repression, ". . . because it was a question of things which the patient wished to forget, and therefore intentionally repressed" (p. 10).

In 1894, force and counterforce were "intolerable sexual ideas" versus the "patient's effort of will":

"These patients whom I analysed had enjoyed good mental health up to the time at which an intolerable idea presented itself within the content of their ideational life; that is to say their ego was confronted by an experience, an idea, a feeling, arousing an affect so painful that the person resolved to forget it, since he had no confidence in his power to resolve the incompatibility between the unbearable idea and his ego by the processes of thought.

"Such unbearable ideas develop in women chiefly in connection with sexual experiences and sensations, and the patients can recollect with the most satisfactory minuteness their efforts at defence — their resolution to 'push things out', not to think of it, to suppress it." (1894, pp. 61–62.)

In this period Freud was convinced that the force always involved sexual experience, though he allowed for the theoretical possibility that this need not invariably be the case: "In all the cases I have analysed it was in the sexual life that a painful affect . . . had originated. On theoretical grounds it is not impossible that this affect may at times arise in other spheres; I have merely to state that hitherto I have not discovered any other origin of it." (1894, p. 66.)

A few years later Freud expressed the antithesis as one between "intolerable ideas" and the "ego": ". . . [the patient's] symptoms arise through . . . an attempt to repress an intolerable idea which was in painful opposition to the patient's ego" (1896, p. 155).

As the account of the seduction theory in the previous chapter shows, the "intolerable ideas" and "strangulated affect" from traumatic experiences were considered to refer to sexual seductions in childhood. The active emotional residues which were the aftermath of these seductions during this period corresponded to the role of force in the final scheme.

FORCE AND THE PREGENITAL SEX THEORY

Of course the force aspect of the antithesis underwent a radical change with the concept of pregenital sex presented in the *Three Essays on the Theory of Sexuality*. The "painful ideas" of the supposed seductions were conceived as screen memories for pregenital sex wishes and for the impulses toward incest of later childhood. This passage added to the *Essays* by Freud in 1915 is an account of the pregenital sex theory:

"The study, with the help of psycho-analysis, of the inhibitions and disturbances of this process of development enables us to recognize abortive beginnings and preliminary stages of a firm organization of the component instincts such as this — preliminary stages which themselves constitute a sexual régime of a sort. These phases of sexual organization are normally passed through smoothly, without giving more than a hint of their existence. It is only in pathological cases that they become active and recognizable to superficial observation.

"We shall give the name of 'pregenital' to organizations of sexual life in which the genital zones have not yet taken over their predominant part. We have hitherto identified two such organizations, which almost seem as though they were harking back to early animal forms of life.

"The first of these is the oral or, as it might be called, cannibalistic pregenital sexual organization. Here sexual activity has not yet been separated from the ingestion of food; nor are opposite currents within the activity differentiated. The *object* of both activities is the same; the sexual *aim* consists in the incorporation of the object — the prototype of a process which, in the form of identification, is later to play such an important psychological part. A relic of this constructed phase of organization, which is forced upon our notice by pathology, may be seen in thumbsucking, in which the sexual activity, detached from the nutritive activity, has substituted for the extraneous object one situated in the subject's own body.

"A second pregenital phase is that of the sadistic-anal organization. Here the opposition between two currents, which runs through all sexual life, is already developed: they cannot yet, however, be described as 'masculine' and 'feminine', but only as 'active' and 'passive'. The *activity* is put into operation by the instinct for mastery through the agency of the somatic musculature; the organ which, more than any other, represents the *passive* sexual aim is the erotogenic mucous membrane of the

103

anus. Both of these currents have objects, which, however, are not identical. Alongside these, other component instincts operate in an auto-erotic manner. In this phase, therefore, sexual polarity and an extraneous object are already observable. But organization and subordination to the reproductive function are still absent." (1905a, pp. 197–99.)

A footnote was added in 1924: "At a later date (1923), I myself modified this account by inserting a third phase in the development of childhood, subsequent to the two pregenital organizations. This phase, which already deserves to be described as genital, presents a sexual object and some degree of convergence of the sexual impulses upon that object; but it is differentiated from the final organization of sexual maturity in one essential respect. For it knows only one kind of genital: the male one. For that reason I have named it the 'phallic' stage of organization." (1905a, footnote to pp. 199–200.)

There were other component instincts in the pregenital period besides the oral, anal, and phallic stages: "It must, however, be admitted that infantile sexual life, in spite of the preponderating dominance of erotogenic zones, exhibits components which from the very first involve other people as sexual objects. Such are the instincts of scopophilia, exhibitionism and cruelty, which appear in a sense independently of erotogenic zones; these instincts do not enter into intimate relations with genital life until later, but are already to be observed in childhood as independent impulses, distinct in the first instance from erotogenic sexual activity." (1905a, pp. 191–92.)

The antiforce in the period of the *Three Essays* consisted of "mental dams" of disgust, shame, and morality: "It is during this period of total or only partial latency that are built up the mental forces which are later to impede the course of the sexual instinct and, like dams, restrict its flow — disgust, feelings of shame, and the claims of aesthetic and moral ideals. . . . On the other hand, these impulses would seem in themselves to be perverse — that is, to arise from erotogenic zones and to derive their activity from instincts which, in view of the direction of the subject's development, can only arouse unpleasurable feelings. They consequently evoke opposing mental forces (reacting impulses) which, in order to suppress this unpleasure effectively, build up the mental dams that I have already mentioned — disgust, shame, and morality." (1905a, pp. 177, 178.)

104

FORCE, COUNTERFORCE, AND THE OEDIPUS COMPLEX

The instinct side of the force versus counterforce scheme reached its most crucial development with the theory of the Oedipus complex, which Freud first described in an 1897 letter to his friend Wilhelm Fliess: "Only one idea of general value has occurred to me. I have found love of the mother and jealousy of the father in my own case too, and now believe it to be a general phenomenon of early childhood. . . . If that is the case, the gripping power of *Oedipus Rex*, in spite of all the rational objections to the inexorable fate that the story presupposes, becomes intelligible . . ." (1954, p. 223.)

The Oedipus complex was shortly described in Freud's *Interpretation of Dreams*: "It is the fate of all of us, perhaps, to direct our first sexual impulse towards our mother and our first hatred and first murderous wish against our father. Our dreams convince us that this is so. King Oedipus, who slew his father Laïus and married his mother Jocasta, merely shows us the fulfilment of our own childhood wishes." (1900, p. 262.)

The antiforce in *The Interpretation of Dreams* was "the force of the repression": ". . . we shrink back from him [King Oedipus] with the whole force of the repression by which those wishes have since been held down within us" (1900, p. 263).

However, at one point in *The Interpretation of Dreams* Freud used "anticathexis," foreshadowing the use to which he was to put this term some fifteen years later: "There then follows a defensive struggle — for the *Pcs.* in turn reinforces its opposition to the repressed thoughts (i.e. produces an 'anticathexis')" (1900, p. 605).

The dream censorship, of course, had the antiforce role in dreamwork: "We can thus plainly see the purpose for which the censorship exercises its office and brings about the distortion of dreams: it does so *in order to prevent the generation of anxiety or other forms of distressing affect*" (1900, p. 267).

EGO INSTINCTS VERSUS SEX INSTINCTS

In 1910 Freud introduced "ego instincts" as a general term for the antiforce and referred to the force side as "the sex instincts": "From the point of view of our attempted explanation, a quite specially important part is played by the undeniable opposition between the instincts which subserve sexuality, the attainment of sexual pleasure, and those other

105

instincts, which have as their aim the self-preservation of the individual — the ego-instincts. . . . The 'ego' feels threatened by the claims of the sexual instincts and fends them off by repressions." (1910, pp. 214, 215.)

The clean-cut opposition between ego instincts and sex instincts soon disappeared when Freud decided, in his 1914 paper on "Narcissism," that parts of the ego instincts were also libidinal. Freud introduced ego instincts and object instincts, both libidinal, in place of his 1910 dichotomy. Finally in the 1920 *Beyond the Pleasure Principle* Freud adopted the opposition of life and death instincts as his great polarity (1920, p. 61).

Neither of these two successors to ego instincts versus sex instincts was a force and counterforce antithesis related to repression and defense. They were polarities and represented oppositions, but the opposition was between two forces, rather than a force and an antiforce. The force and counterforce concept had taken a different path and saw its next and final expression in the concept of instincts versus anticathexis, to which we will now turn.

INSTINCT VERSUS ANTICATHEXIS

At its final, abstract level, the concept of instinct represented the force side of Freud's great polarity, anticathexis the counterforce side.

Instinct. Two important properties of instincts as conceived by Freud are their somatic origins and, particularly, their continuous operation as unceasing pressures:

"By an 'instinct' is provisionally to be understood the psychical representative of an endosomatic, continuously flowing source of stimulation, as contrasted with a 'stimulus', which is set up by *single* excitations coming from *without*" (1905a, p. 168).

"We have now obtained the material necessary for distinguishing between instinctual stimuli and other (physiological) stimuli that operate on the mind. In the first place, an instinctual stimulus does not arise from the external world but from within the organism itself. For this reason it operates differently upon the mind and different actions are necessary in order to remove it. Further, all that is essential in a stimulus is covered if we assume that it operates with a single impact, so that it can be disposed of by a single expedient action. A typical instance of this is motor flight from the source of stimulation. These impacts may, of course, be repeated and summated, but that makes no difference to our notion of the process and to the conditions for the removal of the stimulus. An instinct, on the

106

other hand, never operates as a force giving a *momentary* impact but always as a *constant* one. Moreover, since it impinges not from without but from within the organism, no flight can avail against it. A better term for an instinctual stimulus is a 'need'. What does away with a need is 'satisfaction'. This can be attained only by an appropriate ('adequate') alteration of the internal source of stimulation." (1915a, pp. 118–19.)

It is important to note that this conception of the continuous pressure of instinct stands in contrast to general conceptions of motives found in psychology. Most motivational theorists do not conceive of motives as forces exerting constant pressure, but rather as processes that are usually inactive but can be aroused and that develop pressure under suitable conditions of stimulation. Thus a person with a strong motive toward achievement is not conceived as being under constant pressure from this motive. It may be quite inactive during his vacation with his family and come alive as a motivational pressure when he returns to his office. Freud's conception of instinct does not allow such periods of inactivity. Apparently, at any given moment, a person's life and death instincts exert a constant pressure that is never interrupted for any cause — even sleep. Furthermore, needs as conceived by Freud operate independently of the environment. They are self-contained internal mechanisms that have their own constant energy supply and they press increasingly for discharge regardless of external circumstance. These aspects of Freud's concept of instinct are important not only for consideration of anticathexis, but in discussion of the theory of remoteness in a later chapter.

Anticathexis. We are already familiar with anticathexis from the chapter on resistance, where anticathexis was identified as the general term for the counterforce of which resistance, in its sense of force, is the therapy-room representative.

Conceiving of instinct as a force exerting constant pressure led to a problem in the theory of repression. Since repression as seen in the clinical cases with which Freud was concerned was unsuccessful repression, it did not do away with the instinct: ". . . repression does not hinder the instinctual representative from continuing to exist in the unconscious, from organizing itself further, putting out derivatives and establishing connections. Repression in fact interferes only with the relation of the instinctual representative to *one* psychical system, namely, to that of the conscious." (1915b, p. 149.)

On the contrary, the repressed impulse *grows* in strength and influence by being excluded from awareness: ". . . the instinctual representative develops with less interference and more profusely if it is withdrawn by repression from conscious influence. It proliferates in the dark, as it were, and takes on extreme forms of expression, which when they are translated and presented to the neurotic are not only bound to seem alien to him, but frighten him by giving him the picture of an extraordinary and dangerous strength of instinct. This deceptive strength of instinct is the result of an uninhibited development in phantasy and of the damming-up consequent on frustrated satisfaction." (1915b, p. 149.)

If repression did not alter the constant pressure of instincts, why did not the instincts constantly erupt into consciousness and behavior? One could suppose that this was in fact the case, but that each time this happened the impulse was repressed anew. This would lead to a picture of repression as an endless series of eruptions and repressions. In 1915 Freud solved this problem by assuming the existence of an anti-instinct force, for which he readopted his 1900 term, "anticathexis," and to which he attributed the same property of constant pressure as the instincts possessed, though of course in the opposite direction: "What we require, therefore, is another process which maintains the repression in the first case [in adult repression] and, in the second [primal or childhood repression], ensures its being established, as well as continued. This other process can only be found in the assumption of an *anticathexis*, by means of which the system *Pcs.* [later, the ego] protects itself from the pressure upon it of the unconscious idea." (1915c, p. 181.)

The assumption that both force and counterforce operate as constant pressures makes for a dynamic picture of repression as an endless struggle between the two:

"The process of repression is not to be regarded as an event which takes place *once*, the results of which are permanent, as when some living thing has been killed and from that time onward is dead; repression demands a persistent expenditure of force, and if this were to cease the success of the repression would be jeopardized, so that a fresh act of repression would be necessary. We may suppose that the repressed exercises a continuous pressure in the direction of the conscious, so that this pressure must be balanced by an unceasing counter-pressure. Thus the maintenance of a repression involves an uninterrupted expenditure of force, while its removal results in a saving from an economic point of view." (1915b, p. 151.)

"An important element in the theory of repression is the view that repression is not an event that occurs once but that it requires a permanent expenditure [of energy]. If this expenditure were to cease, the repressed impulse, which is being fed all the time from its sources, would on the next occasion flow along the channels from which it had been forced away, and the repression would either fail in its purpose or would have to be repeated an indefinite number of times. Thus it is because instincts are continuous in their nature that the ego has to make its defensive action secure by a permanent expenditure [of energy]." (1926a, p. 157, translator's brackets.)

Anticathexis is, then, a name for a highly abstract concept. It refers to a hypothesized *force* that has two special properties: 1. Its psychological direction is opposite to that attributed to instincts. 2. It has a constant, uninterrupted character.

This important idea needs to be portrayed in a fuller way for the reader to see the use to which Freud put it and, especially, to see its relationship to his other concepts. This can be done by examining the role of anticathexis in normalcy, sleep, neurosis, and therapy.

In normal development, the ego is divided from the id by a boundary made up of anticathectic forces permanently safeguarding the ego from the instincts: "An investigation of normal, stable states, in which the frontiers of the ego are safeguarded against the id by resistances (or anti-cathexes) and have held firm . . . would teach us little" (1940, p. 46). "The severest demand upon the ego is probably the keeping down of the instinctual claims of the id, and for this end the ego is obliged to maintain great expenditures of energy upon anti-cathexes" (1940, p. 62).

In sleep, there is some diminution of these daytime anticathexes, though some degree of counterforce is maintained even then:

"Sleep is a return of this mind to the womb. Since the waking ego controls the power of movement, that function is paralyzed in sleep, and accordingly a great part of the inhibitions imposed upon the unconscious id become superfluous. The withdrawal or diminution of these anti-cathexes thus allows the id what is now a harmless degree of liberty." (1940, pp. 48–49.)

"Accordingly, too, some amount of the expenditure on repression (anticathexis) would have to be maintained throughout the night, in order to meet the instinctual danger — though the inaccessibility of all paths leading to a release of affect may considerably diminish the height of the anti-cathexis that is necessary" (1917, p. 225).

The role of anticathexes in the neuroses can be seen from the following passages:

"[In obsessional neurosis] the anticathexis from the system *Cs.* comes most noticeably into the foreground. It is this which, organized as a reaction-formation, brings about the first repression." (1915c, p. 185.)

"In anxiety hysteria . . . the cathexis that has taken flight attaches itself to a substitutive idea which, on the one hand, is connected by association with the rejected idea, and, on the other, has escaped repression by reason of its remoteness from that idea. This substitutive idea — a 'substitute by displacement' . . . now plays the part of an anticathexis for the system *Cs.* (*Pcs.*), by securing it against an emergence in the *Cs.* of the repressed idea." (1915c, p. 182.)

"The hysterical anticathexis is mainly directed outwards, against dangerous perceptions. It takes the form of a special kind of vigilance which, by means of restrictions of the ego, causes situations to be avoided that would entail such perceptions, or, if they do occur, manages to withdraw the subject's attention from them." (1926a, p. 158.)

The role of anticathexis in therapy is seen in the following: "With the mention of resistance we have reached the second and more important part of our task. We have already heard that the ego protects itself against the incursion of undesirable elements from the unconscious and repressed id by means of anti-cathexes, which must remain intact if it is to function normally. The more hardly the ego feels itself pressed, the more convulsively it clings (in terror, as it were) to these anti-cathexes, in order to protect what remains of it from further irruptions. But such defensive trends do not by any means harmonize with the aims of our treatment. We desire, on the contrary, that the ego, emboldened by the certainty of our help, shall dare to take the offensive in order to reconquer what has been lost. And it is at this point that we become aware of the strength of these anti-cathexes in the form of *resistances* against our work. The ego shrinks from undertakings that seem dangerous and threaten unpleasure; it must be constantly spurred on and soothed down if it is not to fail us." (1940, pp. 72–73.)

It can be seen that anticathexis is pure counterforce in Freud's theory. In its most abstract sense, it does not even have a content — only an energy and a direction (against instinct). Anticathexis manifests itself in varied specific forms in behavior: as resistance behavior in therapy, as various defenses in neuroses, as a greater impulse freedom in dreams. It is thus the pure force of the repressive tendency itself.

THE MOTIVE OF ANXIETY

While anticathexis represents the force of the repression tendency in its purest form, it is not the final motivational basis for repression. It stands, rather, as a permanent pressure-tendency in an anti-instinct direction which is motivated, fundamentally, by anxiety.

As is well known, Freud had two theories on the relation of anxiety to repression. He first thought that repressed libido turned into anxiety, but later reversed himself and saw anxiety as the cause of repression.

The First Anxiety Theory. Anxiety proved to be a difficult theoretical problem for Freud. In 1894 he developed the idea that, in anxiety neurosis, the libidinal excitation was transformed into anxiety when sex was strongly aroused but not satisfied. He soon adapted the idea to the theory of repression in supposing that repressed libidinal impulses were automatically transformed into anxiety and used this assumption to explain the prominence of anxiety in neuroses. This improbable idea had a remarkably long life and Freud used it for thirty years in his theory of repression. Here are typical quotations from the 1916 period:

"I said that conversion into anxiety, or better, discharge in the form of anxiety, was the immediate fate of libido which encounters repression" (1916–17, p. 355).

"Infantile dread has very little to do with objective anxiety (dread of real danger), but is, on the other hand, closely allied to the neurotic anxiety of adults. It is derived like the latter from undischarged libido." (1916–17, p. 354.)

The 1926 Concept of Anxiety. Freud ascribed these characteristics to anxiety as an emotional state:

"Anxiety, then, is in the first place something that is felt. We call it an affective state, although we are also ignorant of what an affect is. As a feeling, anxiety has a very marked character of unpleasure. But that is not the whole of its quality. Not every unpleasure can be called anxiety, for there are other feelings, such as tension, pain or mourning, which have the character of unpleasure. Thus anxiety must have other distinctive features besides this quality of unpleasure. Can we succeed in understanding the differences between these various unpleasurable affects?

"We can at any rate note one or two things about the feeling of anxiety. Its unpleasurable character seems to have a note of its own — something not very obvious, whose presence is difficult to prove yet which is in all likelihood there. But besides having this special feature which is difficult to isolate, we notice that anxiety is accompanied by fairly definite physical sensations which can be referred to particular organs of the body. As we are not concerned here with the physiology of anxiety, we shall content ourselves with mentioning a few representatives of these sensations. The clearest and most frequent ones are those connected with the respiratory organs and with the heart. They provide evidence that motor innervations — that is, processes of discharge — play a part in the general phenomenon of anxiety.

"Analysis of anxiety-states therefore reveals the existence of (1) a specific character of unpleasure, (2) acts of discharge and (3) perceptions of those acts." (1926a, p. 132–33).

The emotion of anxiety is experienced in situations of *danger*: "If the structure and origin of anxiety are as described, the next question is: what is the function of anxiety and on what occasions is it reproduced? The answer seems to be obvious and convincing: anxiety arose originally as a reaction to a state of *danger* and it is reproduced whenever a state of that kind recurs." (1926a, p. 134.)

Freud went on to discuss the nature of the danger situation and came to distinguish between danger situations that were, at the time of their occurrence, *traumatic* and later *anticipatory* (signal) anxiety responses that functioned as warnings that the once-experienced trauma was threatening to recur:

"We can find out still more about this if, not content with tracing anxiety back to danger, we go on to enquire what the essence and meaning of a danger-situation is. Clearly, it consists in the subject's estimation of his own strength compared to the magnitude of the danger and in his admission of helplessness in the face of it — physical helplessness if the danger is real and psychical helplessness if it is instinctual. In doing this he will be guided by the actual experiences he has had. (Whether he is wrong in his estimation or not is immaterial for the outcome.) Let us call a situation of helplessness of this kind that has been actually experienced a *traumatic situation*. We shall then have a good grounds for distinguishing a traumatic situation from a danger-situation.

"The individual will have made an important advance in his capacity for self-preservation if he can foresee and expect a traumatic situation of this kind which entails helplessness, instead of simply waiting for it to happen. Let us call a situation which contains the determinant for such an expectation a danger-situation. It is in this situation that the signal of anxiety is given. The signal announces: 'I am expecting a situation of helplessness to set in', or: 'The present situation reminds me of one of the traumatic experiences I have had before. Therefore I will anticipate the trauma and behave as though it had already come, while there is yet time to turn it aside.' Anxiety is therefore on one hand an expectation of a trauma, and on the other a repetition of it in a mitigated form. Thus the two features of anxiety which we have noted have a different origin. Its connection with expectation belongs to the danger-situation, whereas its indefiniteness and lack of object belong to the traumatic situation of help-lessness — the situation which is anticipated in the danger-situation.

"Taking this sequence, anxiety-danger-helplessness (trauma), we can now summarize what has been said. A danger-situation is a recognized, remembered, expected situation of helplessness. Anxiety is the original reaction to helplessness in the trauma and is reproduced later on in the danger-situation as a signal for help. The ego, which experienced the trauma passively, now repeats it actively in a weakened version, in the hope of being able itself to direct its course." (1926a, pp. 166–67.)

In this quotation, Freud distinguished "traumatic" anxiety from "signal" or "anticipatory" anxiety, a distinction fundamental to the concepts of primal repression and adult repression. What is the "trauma" that occurs in infancy? "The reason why the infant in arms wants to perceive the presence of its mother is only because it already knows by experience that she satisfies all its needs without delay. The situation, then, which it regards as a 'danger' and against which it wants to be safeguarded is that of non-satisfaction, of a *growing tension due to need*, against which it is helpless." (1926a, p. 137.)

Freud went on to say that traumatic helplessness arising from non-gratification of needs was, in some ways, analogous to the situation of birth. In both cases there was an overwhelming increase in stimuli demanding some disposition.

"Primal" or "traumatic" anxiety, then, is a state of direct, overwhelming helplessness in the face of excessive stimulation. The child soon associatively learns that such traumatic states of non-gratification of need arise in the mother's absence and comes to learn to fear her absence ("object

113

loss"). This is the signal-anxiety mechanism, and later sources of anxiety are also anticipatory in character. The sources of anxiety differ at different periods of life: ". . . we might say that each period of the individual's life has its appropriate determinant of anxiety. Thus the danger of psychical helplessness is appropriate to the period of life when his ego is immature; the danger of loss of object, to early childhood when he is still dependent on others; the danger of castration, to the phallic phase; and the fear of his super-ego, to the latency period. Nevertheless, all these danger-situations and determinants of anxiety can persist side by side and cause the ego to react to them with anxiety at a period later than the appropriate one; or, again, several of them can come into operation at the same time." (1926a, p. 142.)

THE MOTIVATION OF PRIMAL REPRESSION

In the last chapter a distinction was made between primal repression and adult repression. There and in the preceding section of the present chapter, primal repression was related to traumatic anxiety states in infancy, while adult repression was shown to work according to the mechanism of signal anxiety. The repression of developing impulses as a means of *avoiding* potential traumas is an understandable process. But the mechanism of "traumas" and "primal repression" is a puzzle. Seemingly Freud was saying that primal repression was a direct, automatic response to traumas. In other words, apparently, if a state of too intense stimulation occurs in infancy, the infant's *automatic* response is to repress the impulses responsible for this state. How does this happen? What is the mechanism by which this response is accomplished? Freud left the point undiscussed.

Some further light is thrown on this fragmentary theory by Freud's treatment of the idea of trauma and defensive response to excessive stimulation in his *Beyond the Pleasure Principle* of 1920. There (Chapters 4 and 5) Freud constructed an analogy of an organism made of a sensitive substance adapting itself to existence in a world bombarding it with intense stimuli and developing an outer protective layer that screened stimuli, admitting only what could be handled by its limited capacity to control and dispose of (to "bind") stimulation:

"But we have more to say of the living vesicle with its receptive cortical layer. This little fragment of living substance is suspended in the middle of an external world charged with the most powerful energies; and it would be killed by the stimulation emanating from these if it were not

114

provided with a protective shield against stimuli. It acquires the shield in this way: its outermost surface ceases to have the structure proper to living matter, becomes to some degree inorganic and thence-forward functions as a special envelope or membrane resistant to stimuli. In consequence, the energies of the external world are able to pass into the next underlying layers, which have remained living, with only a fragment of their original intensity; and these layers can devote themselves, behind the protective shield, to the reception of the amounts of stimulus which have been allowed through it. By its death, the outer layer has saved all the deeper ones from a similar fate — unless, that is to say, stimuli reach it which are so strong that they break through the protective shield. *Protection against* stimuli is an almost more important function for the living organism than *reception of* stimuli. The protective shield is supplied with its own store of energy and must above all endeavour to preserve the special modes of transformation of energy operating in it against the effects threatened by the enormous energies at work in the external world — effects which tend towards a levelling out of them and hence towards destruction." (1920, p. 27.)

"We have pointed out how the living vesicle is provided with a shield against stimuli from the external world; and we had previously shown that the cortical layer next to that shield must be differentiated as an organ for receiving stimuli from without. This sensitive cortex, however, which is later to become the system *Cs.*, also receives excitations from *within*. The situation of the system between the outside and the inside and the difference between the conditions governing the reception of excitations in the two cases have a decisive effect on the functioning of the system and of the whole mental apparatus. Towards the outside it is shielded against stimuli, and the amounts of excitation impinging on it have only a reduced effect. Towards the inside there can be no such shield; the excitations in the deeper layers extend into the system directly and in undiminished amount, in so far as certain of their characteristics give rise to feelings in the pleasure-unpleasure series. The excitations coming from within are, however, in their intensity and in other, qualitative, respects — in their amplitude, perhaps — more commensurate with the system's method of working than of stimuli which stream in from the external world. This state of things produces two definite results. First, the feelings of pleasure and unpleasure (which are an index to what is happening in the interior of the apparatus) predominate over all external stimuli. And secondly, a particular way is adopted of dealing with any internal excitations which produce too great an increase of unpleasure: there is a tendency to treat them as though they were acting, not from the inside, but from the outside, so that it may be possible to bring the shield against stimuli into operation as a means of defence against them." (1920, pp. 28–29.)

"We describe as 'traumatic' any excitations from outside which are powerful enough to break through the protective shield. It seems to me that the concept of trauma necessarily implies a connection of this kind with a breach in an otherwise efficacious barrier against stimuli. Such an event as an external trauma is bound to provoke a disturbance on a large scale in the functioning of the organism's energy and to set in motion every possible defensive measure. At the same time, the pleasure principle is for the moment put out of action. There is no longer any possibility of preventing the mental apparatus from being flooded with large amounts of stimulus, and another problem arises instead — the problem of mastering the amounts of stimulus which have broken in and of binding them, in the psychical sense, so that they can then be disposed of. . . . And how shall we expect the mind to react to this invasion? Cathectic energy is summoned from all sides to provide sufficiently high cathexes of energy in the environs of the breach. An 'anticathexis' on a grand scale is set up, for whose benefit all the other psychical systems are impoverished, so that the remaining psychical functions are extensively paralysed or reduced." (1920, pp. 29–30.)

"We may, I think, tentatively venture to regard the common traumatic neurosis as a consequence of an extensive breach being made in the protective shield against stimuli" (1920, p. 31).

The analogy so far deals with overintense stimulation from without. Freud notes that the organism is even more helpless against overintense stimuli arising from within (from instinctual impulses) because it has no protective barrier against such inner impulses: "The most abundant sources of this internal excitation are what are described as the organism's 'instincts' — the representatives of all the forces originating in the interior of the body and transmitted to the mental apparatus — at once the most important and the most obscure element of psychological research" (1920, p. 34).

Thus far, we have, in analogical form, the following ideas:

1. The individual can only handle a given quantity of stimulation.

116

2. The external and internal worlds are capable of bombarding the person with stimuli far in excess of the quantity which can be handled without special protective adaptations.

3. The person develops (as a part of his growing ego function) a kind of protective external shield against outer stimuli that regulates the quantity of stimulation that is allowed to affect his internal systems.

4. This protective "shell" can be ruptured under certain conditions: (a) If excessive stimulation occurs under conditions of psychological unpreparedness, rupture can occur. Anticipatory preparation is conceived of (analogically still) as normally working to increase the screening effects of the protective outer shell. Excessive stimulation under unprepared conditions (as in fright) more easily ruptures the defensive shell. (b) If the stimulation is extreme, regardless of preparedness, rupture can occur.

5. A breakdown of the protective mechanism against excessive stimulation gives rise to a "trauma," which, fundamentally, is a state of too great tension arising from the resulting excessive stimulation.

6. Certain pathological states (called "the actual neuroses") were considered by Freud to be direct outcomes of the foregoing processes: (a) the traumatic neuroses of war; (b) the "anxiety neuroses" which he always believed (from 1896 on) to be direct results of excessive sexual stimulation without gratification.

7. The protective mechanism against excessive outer stimuli develops more readily and efficiently than protection against too intense stimulation arising from instinctual sources. This differential efficiency leads the person to treat inner dangers as outer ones in order to take advantage of the better defense against outer stimuli, giving rise to the mechanism of projection.

8. The traumatic anxiety states of infancy, then, are states of extreme tension caused by too intense stimulation when basic needs are not gratified.

What is "primal repression" in relation to such infantile trauma states? If one follows out and applies here Freud's reasoning about the same problem in *Beyond the Pleasure Principle* (where he was concerned with the analogy used above in relation to war neuroses), it would seem that the organism responds to such a breakdown of its protective mechanism against too-intense stimuli by attempting to restore the conditions which existed prior to the traumatic rupture (Chapter 5).

In this work, Freud went on to conclude that such an automatic response occurred because there was a fundamental tendency in life to reinstate the earlier condition, a tendency which had an instinctive basis: "At this point we cannot escape a suspicion that we may have come upon the track of a universal attribute of instincts and perhaps of organic life in general which has not hitherto been clearly recognized or at least not explicitly stressed. *It seems, then, that an instinct is an urge inherent in organic life to restore an earlier state of things* which the living entity has been obliged to abandon under the pressure of external disturbing forces; that is, it is a kind of organic elasticity, or, to put it another way, the expression of the inertia inherent in organic life." (1920, p. 36.)

This instinct to restore earlier conditions is, of course, the "death instinct," or the "constancy" or "Nirvana" principle: "The dominating tendency of mental life, and perhaps of nervous life in general, is the effort to reduce, to keep constant or to remove internal tension due to stimuli (the 'Nirvana principle', to borrow a term from Barbara Low) — a tendency which finds expression in the pleasure principle; and our recognition of that fact is one of our strongest reasons for believing in the existence of death instincts" (1920, pp. 55–56).

Thus it would seem that "primal repression" is a direct, instinctive response to a trauma state, a response which has as its objective the restoration of the condition that existed before the trauma. Since the trauma in "primal" or "traumatic anxiety" states of infancy comes from too intense stimulation due to inner tensions arising from non-gratification of needs, the organism responds automatically by "repressing" the instincts responsible for the extreme tension. This process is "primal repression." Its motivation is the instinctive tendency to repetition (repetition-compulsion), which has the death instinct as its ultimate source.

This innate reaction, which becomes manifest as anticathexis, is the counterforce in the case of primal repression: "Anticathexis is the sole mechanism of primal repression, in the case of repression proper ('after-pressure') there is in addition withdrawal of the *Pcs.* cathexis" (1915b, p. 181).

The motive behind the anticathectic force, then, differs in primal and adult repression. In primal repression it is an innate tendency to reinstate an earlier condition (constancy principle); while in adult repression, the person's anticipatory anxiety that the childhood traumas will recur is the motive behind the anticathectic force.

MOTIVES OF REPRESSION AND DEFENSE

REPRESSIBLE MOTIVES

The foregoing discussion of the motivational basis of primal repression established that such repression is an instinctive response, an instance of a pure counterforce or anticathexis having innate origins. While this abstract idea has considerable interest to the theoretician, there is an even more important motivational implication of the concept of primal repression for the theory of repression.

As seen in the last chapter on the theory of primal repression, adults respond repressively only if they have once before done so at a period in life when their personalities were too immature to cope with states of overwhelming stimulation (traumas). This is a general statement of the essential dependence on childhood repressive responses and similar responses in later years. Freud's theory of repression is more specific than this. Not only is there this relation of dependence between inadequate response mechanisms at the two periods in life, but the *content* of what was repressed in the two periods is similarly related. If we call the repressible motives of infancy and childhood "primal motives," Freud's theory was that adult motives were repressible *only* to the extent that they were associatively connected with primal motives. Of course, in Freud's motivational theory, the "primal motives" were the pregenital and incestuous impulses. This means, then, that adult motives and ideas are repressible *only* insofar as their content has the power to rearouse, or threaten to rearouse, primal motives. In other words, only adult material that can rearouse pregenital or incest motives is repressible.

This formulation of Freud's gives the theory of repression a motivational specificity that we are not accustomed to employ in contemporary usage of the word "repression." One of the main post-Freudian developments concerning repression has been an extension of the concept to cover motives of all kinds. This extension has become such an everyday assumption that most workers in psychoanalysis today who consider themselves to be working within the basic Freudian theory express surprised disbelief if told that their current formulations are ones that Freud would not have agreed with. From the first, and unswervingly to the end, Freud insisted that only primal motives or materials associatively connected with primal motives are repressible. Even hostility is repressible only because of its associative connections with primal motives.

To establish this point, let us look in turn at the three main motives of Freud's theory, anxiety, sex, and hostility, in their relation to repression.

119

Anxiety and Repression. Since this relationship has been thoroughly discussed, it remains only to point out that the *intensity* of the anxiety aroused is a factor in repression. Freud never made any quantitative statement on this point but a check of some of his cases shows them to be involved in rather drastic threat situations compared with what is seen in attempted laboratory analogues of repression. Consider these examples:

Katharina was a girl of eighteen whose uncle had tried to seduce her at fourteen. She later (age sixteen) saw him seduce her cousin and she betrayed him to his wife. The uncle angrily threatened her. (1895, pp. 125–34.)

Elizabeth R., a very moral girl, found herself in love with her sister's husband. The sister died, leaving her free to marry her brother-in-law. (1895, pp. 135–82.)

Frau P.'s problems centered around an incestuous relationship with her older brother from childhood to age eleven (1896, pp. 169–82).

Dora was an eighteen-year-old girl in love with Herr K., a married man with children. Herr K.'s wife simultaneously was mistress to her own father. Herr K. tried to seduce Dora. (1905b, pp. 7–122.)

When one recalls that these manifest conditions are signal-anxiety states that have profoundly traumatic meanings stemming from overwhelming infantile and childhood experiences, it is clear that anxiety in clinical repression is a very intense motivational state — so extreme in fact as to raise the question whether artificial production of such states in laboratory research is possible.

Freud's own statement on the intensity of motivation in repression is that repressible ideas (in the sense of primally associated ideas) will not be repressed under mild motivational conditions. The objectionable impulses must attain a certain intensity before repression occurs:

"Finally, we must not forget that after all we have said very little about an instinctual impulse when we have established that it is repressed. Without prejudice to its repression, such an impulse may be in widely different states. It may be inactive, i.e. only very slightly cathected with mental energy; or it may be cathected in varying degrees, and so enabled to be active. True, its activation will not result in a direct removal of the repression, but it will set in motion all the processes which end in a penetration by the impulse into consciousness along circuitous paths. With unrepressed derivatives of the unconscious the fate of a particular idea is often decided by the degree of its activity or cathexis. It is an everyday occurrence that such a derivative remains unrepressed so long as it represents only a small amount of energy, although its content would be calculated to give rise to a conflict with what is dominant in consciousness. The quantitative factor proves decisive for this conflict: as soon as the basically obnoxious idea exceeds a certain degree of strength, the conflict becomes a real one, and it is precisely this activation that leads to repression." (1915b, pp. 151–52.)

Sex and Repression. Anxiety, of course, is only one facet of the motivational side of repression. Simply unbearable anxiety or tension will not, in itself, lead to repression:

"Let us take the case in which an instinctual stimulus such as hunger remains unsatisfied. It then becomes imperative and can be allayed by nothing but the action that satisfies it; it keeps up a constant tension of need. Nothing in the nature of a repression seems in this case to come remotely into question.

"Thus repression certainly does not arise in cases where the tension produced by lack of satisfaction of an instinctual impulse is raised to an unbearable degree." (1915b, p. 147.)

For effective repression, not only must there be a state of high tension, but the tension must be associated with a threat to one's self-esteem. This point has been recognized in the research techniques which use such ego-insult procedures as implying that the subject is extremely unintelligent, or that he is "imbalanced" in personality. Here researchers and Freud would seem to agree: "Repression, we have said, proceeds from the ego; we might say with greater precision that it proceeds from the self-respect of the ego. The same impressions, experiences, impulses and desires that one man indulges or at least works over consciously will be rejected with the utmost indignation by another, or even stifled before they enter consciousness. The difference between the two, which contains the conditioning factor of repression, can easily be expressed in terms which enable it to be explained by the libido theory. We can say that the one man has set up an *ideal* in himself by which he measures his actual ego, while the other had formed no such ideal. For the ego the formation of an ideal would be the conditioning factor of repression." (1914b, pp. 93–94.)

But can the threat to one's picture of the self as an intelligent or normal person be assumed to be equivalent to a threat to self-esteem in the areas of personality with which Freud's theory was concerned? It is clear that Freud limited the use of repression responses strictly to threats to self-esteem arising from *sexual or sex-associated motivation*. He never once veered from his insistence that sexual motivation is basic to neuroses (and hence to repression). His statement of 1922 is explicit on this point: "None of the theses of psycho-analysis has met with such tenacious scepticism or such embittered resistance as this assertion of the preponderating aetiological significance of sexual life in the neuroses. It should, however, be expressly remarked that, in its development up to the present day, psycho-analysis has found no reason to retreat from this opinion." (1922, p. 243.)

Of course, "sex" here covers pregenital and incest motives (primal motives), as well as genital sex. This aspect of Freud's theory was reviewed earlier in the chapter. If we lump all that Freud considered to be pregenital and Oedipal motives together as "primal motives," we may say that primal repression is a direct, automatic response to states of childhood helplessness resulting from the too intense stimulation that accompanies the operation of such primal motives. Only adult motives that have the power to rearouse these primal impulses can result in adult repression. Genital sex can arouse such potent reminders of primal experiences in childhood, Freud said, because it is inherently a part of the same complex of innate instinctive impulses that pregenital impulses belong to.

Hostility and Repression. The repression of hostility has the same status as the repression of adult sex: it must be associatively connected to primal impulses that were repressed in childhood. Hostility is not, in and of itself, a repressible motive in Freud's theory. Even Freudian scholars are inclined to question this point and it is worth documenting in detail.

Although hostility was not given major attention in Freud's theory until *Beyond the Pleasure Principle* in 1920, he took hostility into account very early and continued to be concerned with it throughout. The briefly held theory of sex seduction was the earliest instance in which a systematic role was given to hostility. Here the primacy of sex and the associative status of hostility in repression were clear: "In the aetiology of the obsessional neurosis sexual experiences in early childhood play the same part as in hysteria; it is here, however, no longer a question of sexual passivity, but rather of aggressive acts performed with pleasure and of pleasurable participation in sexual acts — of sexual activity, therefore. . . . The nature of the obsessional neurosis permits of description in a simple formula — *Obsessions are always reproaches re-emerging in a transmuted form under*

122

repression — reproaches which invariably relate to a sexual deed performed with pleasure in childhood." (1896, p. 162.)

In his treatment of cruelty as a motive in his 1905 *Three Essays on the Theory of Sexuality* Freud linked it intimately to sex both in his assumption that children have an innate "component instinct" of cruelty, and in his analysis of sadism in perversions. In the case of the "component instinct" of cruelty, he supposed that it was at first quite independent of sex but soon it became firmly associated with the erogenous impulses: "It may be assumed that the impulses of cruelty arise from sources which are in fact independent of sexuality, but may become united with it at an early stage owing to an anastomosis [cross-connection] near their points of origin. Observation teaches us, however, that sexual development and the development of the instinct of scopophilia and cruelty are subject to mutual influences which limit this presumed independence of the two sets of instincts." (1905a, p. 193, footnote 1, translator's bracketed insertion.)

In sadism the intimate connection between sex and aggression is revealed in a particularly direct form: "Thus sadism would correspond to an aggressive component of the sexual instinct which has become independent and exaggerated and, by displacement, has usurped the leading position . . . The history of human civilization shows beyond any doubt that there is an intimate connection between cruelty and the sexual instinct . . . " (1905a, pp. 158–59.)

In the 1913–15 period Freud continued to consider hostility mainly as observed in the obsessional neuroses: "The extraordinary part played by impulses of hatred and anal erotism in the symptomatology of obsessional neurosis has already struck many observers and has recently been emphasized with particular clarity by Ernest Jones" (1913, p. 321).

In fact it was the prominence of hostility in such cases that led to the assumption of a sadistic-anal stage: "On the contrary, the component instincts which dominate this *pregenital organization* of sexual life are the anal-erotic and sadistic ones" (1913, p. 321).

The repression of hostility was clearly recognized, but it was *sex-linked* hostility: ". . . in *obsessional neurosis* . . . we are at first in doubt what it is that we have to regard as the instinctual representative that is subjected to repression — whether it is a libidinal or a hostile trend. This uncertainty arises because obsessional neurosis has as its basis a regression owing to which a sadistic trend has been substituted for an affectionate

123

one. It is this hostile impulsion against someone who is loved which is subjected to repression." (1915b, p. 156.)

Finally, of course, Freud gave the aggressive instinct a separate and independent status from sex:

"In all that follows I take up the standpoint that the tendency to aggression is an innate, independent, instinctual disposition in man . . ." (1930, p. 102).

"I know that we have always had before our eyes manifestations of the destruction instinct fused with erotism directed outwards and inwards in sadism and masochism; but I can no longer understand how we could have overlooked the universality of non-erotic aggression and destruction" (1930, p. 99).

The recognition of nonsexual aggression would appear, finally, to clear the way for the possibility that hostility as such is an independently repressible motive. However, there is no support for such a view in Freud's writings. He continued to the end to insist that, in his experience, he always found hostility to be associated with sex. In a discussion of Eros and the death instinct, he said: "From this example one could then surmise that the two kinds of instincts seldom — perhaps never — appear in isolation, but always mingle with each other in different, very varying proportions, and so made themselves unrecognizable to us" (1930, p. 98).

"The name libido can again be used to denote the manifestations of the power of Eros in contradistinction to the energy of the death instinct. We must confess that it is more difficult to detect the latter, and to a great extent we can merely conjecture its existence as a background to Eros, also that it eludes us whenever it is not betrayed by a fusion with Eros." (1930, p. 101.)

"Our present point of view can be roughly expressed in the statement that libido participates in every instinctual manifestation, but that not everything in that manifestation is libido" (1930, footnote, p. 101).

"Fortunately the instincts of aggression are never alone, they are always alloyed with the erotic ones" (1933, p. 152).

Close reading of the passages from which these quotations are drawn leads to the conclusion that Freud from 1896 onward gave a major role to sex-associated hostility in repression, particularly in obsessional cases and sadism, and finally came to recognize the theoretical existence of a separate hostility motive not linked to sex. He insisted, however, that the two, while conceptually independent, are never clinically separate, that

124

hostility that is not associated with sex cannot even be observed by psycho-analytic methods. If one remembers that "associated with sex" means "associated with pregenital sex or incest," it becomes clear that aggression, like adult sexuality, has to be associatively connected with these "primal impulses" of childhood to be repressible.

In *Moses and Monotheism*, Freud discussed the motives that were involved in primal repression: "[The traumatic experiences of early childhood which underlie neuroses] concern impressions of a sexual and aggressive nature and also early injuries to the self (injuries to narcissism). It should be added that children at that early age do not yet distinguish between sexual and purely aggressive actions so clearly as they do later on (the 'sadistic' misunderstanding of the sexual act belongs to this context). It is of course very striking that the sexual factor should predominate, and theory must take this into account." (1939, pp. 116–17.)

Here, in one of his very last writings, the primary role of sex and aggression in repression, as well as the idea of their close interconnection, is stated plainly. He also introduces a third motive: "early injuries to the self (injuries to narcissism)." Presumably "narcissism" is associated with sex in this case as well.

SUMMARY

The underlying theoretical structure of the theory of repression and defense is motivational. In the most abstract terms the conception poses a force opposed by a counterforce. The final terminology of this motivational antithesis was "instinct" versus "anticathexis," but there were many intervening developments and a complex relation to anxiety at the end.

Some early terms and concepts that Freud used for the antithesis of force and counterforce can best be summarized schematically:

Force	Counterforce
Distressing antithetic ideas	Self-confidence
Counter-will	Will
Strangulated affect	Repression tendency
Intolerable sexual ideas	Will, Efforts at defense
Intolerable ideas	Ego's attempt to repress
Childhood seductions	Repression tendency
Pregenital sex impulses	Disgust, shame, morality
Incest wishes	Force of repression
Repressed thoughts	Anticathexis, Dream censor
Sex instincts	Ego instincts

125

The instincts (the force) were assumed to have somatic origins and to act as constant forces pressing for expression in consciousness and behavior. Instincts are self-energizing, being independent of environmental stimulation. The conception that instincts exert constant pressure led Freud to assume that repression must work as a constant counterpressure. In 1915 he reinstituted an early term, "anticathexis" as a name for this constant counterforce and thereafter used it frequently.

In normal persons, the ego is separated from the id by a constant anticathectic force that acts as a barrier against the instincts of the id. This anticathexis is maintained to some extent even in sleep, though at a much lower level that allows instinctual expression in dreams. In neuroses, the anticathexis takes the form of various defenses such as reaction-formation, displacement, and ego-restriction. In therapy the anticathectic force appears in the guise of resistances.

Anticathexis is pure counterforce. It represents a quantity of energy with a certain direction (opposed to instinct), but has no fixed content. This counterforce becomes manifest in certain situations that do have a characteristic behavioral content, such as resistance behavior, defense, or greater impulse expression in dreams, but in its most abstract form it is the pure force of the repression tendency.

In adult repression the constant counterforce of anticathexis has its ultimate origins in anxiety. Freud had two theories of anxiety. The first, which he maintained for thirty years, was that anxiety came from repressed libido. In 1926 he reversed himself and saw anxiety as the underlying motive for repression.

The final theory of anxiety had a complex structure because it had aspects concerning both adults and children, just as the theory of sex had. Adult anxiety, Freud said, was "signal anxiety," an anticipation that traumas suffered in childhood would recur if instinctual impulses were not counter-cathected. Freud called the anxiety of childhood "traumatic anxiety" and said that, fundamentally, it is a state of overwhelming psychic helplessness.

The traumatic anxiety of childhood has different origins at different ages:

1. The earliest traumas of infancy are states of overwhelming helplessness due to non-gratification of physical needs.

2. Later, separation from the mother becomes a source of traumas,

since the child has learned that the mother's absence is a signal that traumas of physical need are likely to recur.

3. Castration threat is the great trauma of the Oedipal period.

These "primal traumas" of infancy and childhood are necessary forerunners of adult anxiety, Freud said. After the formation of the superego (coincident with the repression of the Oedipus complex), anxiety becomes "signal anxiety," an anticipation that primal traumas will recur.

The motivation of primal repression is obscure, but a convincing picture can be put together from Freud's psychology of traumas portrayed in *Beyond the Pleasure Principle* and various scattered suggestions. These yield the following explanations:

1. The individual is capable of handling only a limited quantity of stimulation, either from without or from within.

2. Both the external and internal worlds at times bombard the person with stimuli far in excess of what he can handle without special protective mechanisms.

3. The person develops such a protective mechanism in the form of a barrier shield that regulates stimulation; a kind of "shell" develops as a part of ego development.

4. This protective ego-shell can be ruptured under certain conditions such as the excessive stimulation of war, strong but ungratified arousal of sexual desires, and, particularly, the traumas of infancy and childhood.

5. When such a rupture due to the overtension coming from excessive stimulation develops, there is a primitive, innate, automatic reaction which attempts to restore the pre-trauma state.

6. Fundamentally, this instinctive attempt to restore an earlier condition reflects the tendency to repeat that Freud found to be basic to all psychic and even biological life, and that he named the death instinct.

7. Thus, the motivation for primal repression is an automatic, innate, instinctive response to a condition of overstimulation, a response that tends to restore the pre-trauma state. It is the same tendency that Freud postulated to explain repetition in battle dreams, children's play, transference, and life in general.

The motivation of primal repression, then, differs from that of adult repression in that its anticathectic force has its basis in an instinctive response, while in adult repression the anticathexis is kept up because of anticipatory anxiety that the primal traumas of infancy and childhood will recur if instincts are not counter-cathected.

127

The development of the anxiety theory as a two-stage process in which adult response has its basis in childhood not only paralleled the structure of the concept of primal repression but allowed a completion of Freud's long line of thought about childhood repressions being essential prerequisites to adult repression. Childhood or primal repressions are responses to the primal traumas of that period, and adult repression is based upon these through the warning by the signal-anxiety mechanism of the danger of recurrence of primal traumas if adult sexual impulses are not anticathected.

Adult sex is not really what the neurotic fears. His apprehension comes from the fear that childhood traumas will recur. Adult sex is simply a reminder of these primal traumas, since the most important primal trauma is the castration threat of the Oedipal period. The Oedipal impulses and the outcome of the whole complex, in turn, depend upon earlier pregenital fixations and traumas associated with them. In Freud's theory the castration trauma is necessarily linked to the whole history of the person's pregenital sex experiences. Adult sex is dangerous because, through the mechanism of signal anxiety, and through the associative connections between adult sex, castration fears, and the whole pregenital period, adult sex means childhood sexual traumas.

Not only is it true, then, that adult repressions rest upon childhood repressions as their essential precondition, but adult sex is only repressible insofar as it has associative connections with childhood sex (incestuous and pregenital). That is, adult sex is not repressible *as such*, but *only* through its associative connections with childhood sex.

Hostility has exactly the same status in Freud's theory of repression. It is not repressible as such, but only through its associative connection with childhood sex. Freud had always considered aggression to be associated with sex, as shown in his treatment of this motive from the theory of sex seduction (the seductions were aggressive) through the development of the concept of pregenital sex in which aggression was conceived as one of the components of pregenital sex in the form of an innate tendency to cruelty. This originally independent tendency toward aggression, Freud said, always became linked to sex so inevitably that it could be regarded as one of the sexual impulses of the pregenital period. When Freud later recognized the aggressive instinct as a motive separate and independent from sex, it seemed logical that he would also regard it as being repressible as a motive independent of sex. His later writings do not explicitly affirm

128

or deny that hostility is a repressible motive as such. However, he insists that, although independent in origin, hostility is *always* associated with sex in psychological experience. It follows from this that repressed hostility, too, is invariably associated with sex.

The same conclusion on the independent repressibility of hostility follows from the concept of primal repression. Since the important primal motives are pregenital or incestuous, in Freud's theory, and only adult motives that rearouse these primal traumas of childhood are repressible, adult hostility, like adult sex, would have to have associative connections with the primally repressed incestuous and pregenital motives of infancy and childhood to be repressible in adulthood. The same would be true of *any* repressible adult motive in Freud's theory.

VIII

Remoteness and Repression

A MOST important aspect of the theory of repression is Freud's idea that repressed material can be represented in consciousness under certain conditions – providing the material is in a form that does not permit ego recognition. If the true meaning of a repressed impulse is hidden from the person because of such remoteness, the otherwise objectionable motive can enter awareness.

There are three main types of remoteness: defensive misrepresentations of impulses, expression of symptoms, and situational remoteness. The latter includes dreams, free association, daytime fantasies, and jokes.

DEFENSIVE MISREPRESENTATIONS AS REMOTENESS

We are already acquainted with repressive defenses as responses that achieve repression through misrepresentation of impulses in consciousness. Although Freud did not clearly identify them as such, all defensive distortions of impulse are instances of remoteness in which some aspects of the repressed impulse are present in awareness but in a form that misrepresents their true character.* Isolation is a notable instance. In the famous "rat-man" case, for example, the patient was, from the first, conscious of the murderous wishes toward his father that were at the base of his problems, but they were present in only an intellectual form, deprived of their emotional impact by inhibition of the affective aspect of the impulses. Negation is a further example; a statement such as "I *don't* want to kill my mother" was considered by Freud to be the distorted form of "I *do* want to kill my mother" (1925a). By denying the impulse, the impulse itself can be in consciousness.

* This is true of all the repressive defenses except amnesia.

REMOTENESS AND REPRESSION

SYMPTOMS AS REMOTE EXPRESSIONS OF REPRESSED IMPULSES

In Freud's theory, symptoms are doubly determined. They are the outcome of both the force and the counterforce: ". . . the symptom is supported not only by this anticathexis but also by the instinctual cathexis from the system *Ucs.* which is condensed in the symptom" (1915c, p. 185).

The status of symptoms as distorted representations of the instincts is revealed in passages such as the following:

"For the symptom, being the true substitute for and derivative of the repressed impulse, carries on the role of the latter; it continually renews its demands for satisfaction and thus obliges the ego in its turn to give the signal of unpleasure and put itself in a posture of defence" (1926a, p. 100).

"A symptom is a sign of, and a substitute for, an instinctual satisfaction which has remained in abeyance; it is a consequence of the process of repression" (1926a, p. 91).

"A symptom arises from an instinctual impulse which has been detrimentally affected by repression. If the ego, by making use of the signal of unpleasure, attains its object of completely suppressing the instinctual impulse, we learn nothing of how this has happened. We can only find out about it from those cases in which repression must be described as having to a greater or less extent failed. In this event the position, generally speaking, is that the instinctual impulse has found a substitute in spite of repression, but a substitute which is very much reduced, displaced and inhibited and which is no longer recognizable as a satisfaction." (1926a, pp. 94–95.)

SITUATIONAL REMOTENESS

It is the third type of remoteness that is of the greatest interest. The basic idea is that, under special situational conditions, ordinarily repressed impulses will become manifest. Here are some of the passages in which Freud described the varieties of situational remoteness:

"Reverting once more, however, to the opposite aspect of repression, let us make it clear that it is not even correct to suppose that repression withholds from the conscious *all* the derivatives of what was primally repressed. If these derivatives have become sufficiently far removed from the repressed representative, whether owing to the adoption of distortions or by reason of the number of intermediate links inserted, they have free

131

access to the conscious. It is as though the resistance of the conscious against them was a function of their distance from what was originally repressed. In carrying out the technique of psycho-analysis, we continually require the patient to produce such derivatives of the repressed as, in consequence either of their remoteness or of their distortion, can pass the censorship of the conscious. Indeed, the associations which we require him to give without being influenced by any conscious purposive idea and without any criticism, and from which we reconstitute a conscious translation of the repressed representative — these associations are nothing else than remote and distorted derivatives of this kind . . . Neurotic symptoms, too, must have fulfilled this same condition, for they are derivatives of the repressed, which has, by their means, finally won the access to consciousness which was previously denied to it.

"We can lay down no general rule as to what degree of distortion and remoteness is necessary before the resistance on the part of the conscious is removed . . . it is a question of calling a halt when the cathexis of the unconscious reaches a certain intensity — an intensity beyond which the unconscious would break through to satisfaction." (1915b, pp. 149–50.)

Freud went on to point to the telling of jokes as a condition of remoteness under which repressed material may become conscious:

"The same result as follows from an increase or decrease in the degree of distortion may also be achieved . . . by a modification in the condition for the production of pleasure and unpleasure. Special techniques have been evolved, with the purpose of bringing about such changes in the play of mental forces that what would otherwise give rise to unpleasure may on this occasion result in pleasure; and, whenever a technical device of this sort comes into operation, the repression of an instinctual representative which would otherwise be repudiated is removed. These techniques have till now only been studied in any detail in jokes. As a rule the repression is only temporarily removed and is promptly reinstated." (1915b, pp. 150–51.)

Sleep and dreaming are conditions of remoteness: "The mobility of repression, incidentally, also finds expression in the psychical characteristics of the state of sleep, which alone renders possible the formation of dreams. With a return to waking life the repressive cathexes which have been drawn in are once more sent out." (1915b, p. 151.)

Daytime fantasies too can express ordinarily repressed impulses providing they are not intensely cathected: "In brief, it must be said that the *Ucs.* is continued into what are known as derivatives . . .

"Among the derivatives of the *Ucs.* instinctual impulses, of the sort we have described, there are some which unite in themselves characters of an opposite kind. On the one hand, they are highly organized, free from self-contradiction, have made use of every acquisition of the system Cs. and would hardly be distinguished in our judgment from the formations of that system. On the other hand they are unconscious and are incapable of becoming conscious. Thus *qualitatively* they belong to the system *Pcs.*, but factually to the *Ucs.* . . . . Of such a nature are those phantasies of normal people as well as of neurotics which we have recognized as preliminary stages in the formation both of dreams and of symptoms and which, in spite of their high degree of organization, remain repressed and therefore cannot become conscious. They draw near to consciousness and remain undisturbed so long as they do not have an intense cathexis, but as soon as they exceed a certain height of cathexis they are thrust back." (1915c, pp. 190–91.)

There is a concept expressed in such words as "derivatives," "remoteness," "distance," "distortion," a concept that was clearly present in Freud's thinking but was not explicitly named and developed by him. This idea might be called "a gradient of remoteness," and Freud came nearest to expressing it when he said: "It is as though the resistance of the conscious against them [the derivatives, that is] was a function of their distance from what was originally repressed."

The least degree of remoteness, of course, would be the consciously recognized acceptance of the originally repressed impulse expressed without disguise of any kind. From this pole of *direct* acceptance and expression of impulse there runs a gradient of increasingly disguised and psychologically more distant or indirect expressions of impulse. Such indirect expressions of impulses are "derivatives." Symptoms, defensive distortions, dreams, fantasies, jokes, and free associations are "derivatives" in this sense.

The idea of a remoteness gradient is of particular interest for the problem of trying to measure repression tendency. It will be seen that the difference between the extent of expression of impulse under less remote conditions and the extent of expression under more remote conditions would constitute one basis for developing measures of repression tendency, a possibility which will be taken up in detail in a later chapter.

133

As a final point on the concept of situational remoteness, its dependence on several other Freudian assumptions should be pointed out.

First, the appearance of impulses under conditions of remoteness depends upon their assumed character as continuous forces. Under normal conditions, as we have seen, this constant pressure of instincts is balanced by the constant counterpressure of anticathexis. Remoteness is basically a condition under which the force of anticathexis is lowered, as in sleep. The reason the normally repressed impulses are held to appear with a lowering of the counterforce is essentially that, being forces whose nature it is to press constantly for expression, they will naturally and inevitably do so as soon as the anticathexis is lowered. Under conditions where the ego is deceived as to the true character of the impulse expression, it lowers the anticathectic barrier and expression of impulse automatically takes place.

Second, the appearance of impulses under conditions of remoteness depends upon the assumption that instincts are self-energizing, self-contained motives that receive their impulsion from within the person *independently* of what the environment happens to be. In Freud's conception of instinct, the environment does not act as a stimulus to the arousal of need. Need is self-arousing. It moves the person to deal with his environment in such a way as to satisfy the instinct, but environment does not initiate need.

These two assumptions, that instincts exert a continuous force and that they are independent of environment, have been widely made in the theory and use of projective tests, although the presence of the assumptions has usually been unrecognized. Thus, projective tests attempt to create conditions of remoteness. The user assumes that if the person is engaged in an activity such as telling stories or interpreting ink blots so that he does not recognize the implications of his productions, normally repressed impulses will become manifest. If such impulses act as constant forces, any situation of remoteness will necessarily release them.

The relative inattention paid to the nature of the stimulus in projective tests follows from the idea that the instinct does not depend on the environment for its arousal, and from confidence that the constant pressure of the instinct will force it to appear if the situation is unstructured enough.

A later chapter on measurement will deal further with these matters; the issue is raised here to show the general importance of the concept of remoteness.

134

SUMMARY

A particularly interesting aspect of Freud's theory of repression that has come into wide prominence with the development of projective testing is his idea that impulses which are normally repressed can be conscious under conditions where the ego cannot see their true meaning. He called these "remoteness" conditions. Three types of remoteness can be distinguished: defensive misrepresentations of impulse, symptoms, and situational remoteness (dreams, free association, daytime fantasies, and jokes).

Defensive misrepresentation of impulses is clearly a remoteness condition, although Freud only indirectly mentioned this possibility. All the defenses called "repressive defenses" in Chapter I except amnesia would qualify as such remote expressions of repressed impulses. Thus, in isolation, a patient can be conscious of murderous impulses provided their affective component is inhibited. In negation, the repressed impulse can be conscious provided it is stated as a denial: "I *don't* want to hurt anybody."

Symptoms were explicitly considered to be instances of remote expression of impulses by Freud. He regarded symptoms as direct substitutes for repressed impulses and as actual representatives of the impulse. Thus, a neurotic symptom in Freudian theory necessarily is, in part, a disguised sexual, pregenital, or incestual impulse, or one associatively connected with such impulses.

In their remaining part, symptoms express the force of the anticathexis. They are prohibitions as well as gratifications, being jointly determined by both the force and the counterforce.

The various types of situational remoteness are of the greatest interest. Dreaming is the historic Freudian example in which otherwise repressed impulses appear because a dream is remote from the danger of ego recognition of its true meaning. Free association is the most used remoteness condition in psychoanalysis. The person is placed in a special situation where normal taboos are lifted. He is told that his thoughts need not make sense and urged to tell all. The resulting senseless (to the patient) character of his productions conceal their meaning sufficiently from the ego to allow remote expression of repressed impulses. These are picked up by the analyst and used in his diagnosis and treatment of the patient.

Daytime fantasies, Freud said, have the same character. Repressed impulses can express themselves in such fantasies as long as the ego does not pay attention to them. If we start examining them, we find the task extremely difficult because our resistances arise at once as the normal anticathectic barrier of the ego against instinct is resumed because of the danger of ego recognition.

Wit, humor, and joking were seen by Freud as forms in which impulses are expressed remotely through culturally standardized patterns. Under these conditions, the ego is kept from recognizing that the unacceptable motives involved belong to the person himself.

The concept of situational remoteness directly implies a *gradient* of remoteness ranging from less to more remote conditions of impulse expression. Such an idea leads to the possibility of measuring repression tendency through differences in impulse expression under less and more remote conditions. Freud implicitly used such an estimate of repression tendency in his comparisons of impulse expression evident in the patient's life history (less remote) with impulse expression evident in free association or dreams (more remote).

The concept of remoteness is dependent on two other Freudian assumptions about instinct. The automatic appearance of impulses under remoteness conditions depends upon Freud's conception of instincts as continuous forces and upon the assumption that instincts are self-energizing, independent of environmental arousal. Both of these assumptions enter into the theory and use of projective tests in psychology.

PART TWO · THE THEORETICAL AND
OBSERVATIONAL LANGUAGE

✶ Prologue to Part Two

THE preceding chapters have attempted a complete representation of Freud's theory of repression and defense. In the chapters of Part Two we shall try to build on this foundation in working toward a solution of some of the difficulties that scientists and philosophers of science have found with psychoanalytic theory, of which the concept of repression and defense is so central a part.

These difficulties are summarized in the following passages by a psychologist (Gardner Lindzey) and a philosopher (Ernest Nagel):

"There are many *formal shortcomings* to psychoanalysis as a body of theory, and these shortcomings pose a striking problem for the person who wishes to use the theory as a means of generating ideas for investigation. It is clear that initially there is a lack of satisfactory *coordinating definitions* for the empirical concepts of the theory. That is, there is no provision for the necessary steps whereby the theoretical statements can be translated into the world of reality or observation. Just what is the empirical referent of oral fixation, castration anxiety, primary narcissism, or genital adjustment? The literature contains many statements that are relevant to the empirical translation of these concepts, but these statements are by no means adequately explicit, nor are they ever completely consistent among themselves. Furthermore, most of the discussions are concerned with relating psychoanalytic concepts to events in the psychoanalytic interview and consequently are of little use in the attempt to apply the theory to other domains of behavior." (15, p. 11.)

"Freudian theory maintains, and I think rightly so, that it is not possible to account for most human conduct exclusively in terms either of manifest human traits or of conscious motives and intentions. Accordingly, the theory introduces a number of assumptions containing terms that ostensibly refer to matters neither manifest nor conscious, and that are not explicitly definable by way of what is manifest and conscious. In so far as Freudian theory employs notions of this kind which do not describe anything observable (let me call such notions 'theoretical' ones for the sake of brevity), the theory is quite like the molecular theory of gases or the gene theory of heredity. I do not think, therefore, that there is any substance in those criticisms of Freudian theory which object to the theory *merely* on the ground that it uses theoretical notions.

"a) My first difficulty with Freudian theory nevertheless is generated by the fact that while it is unobjectionable for a theory to be couched in terms of theoretical notions, the theory does not seem to me to satisfy two requirements which any theory must satisfy if it is to be capable of empirical validation. I must state these requirements briefly. In the first place, it must be possible to deduce determinate consequences from the assumptions of theory, so that one can decide on the basis of logical considerations, and prior to the examination of any empirical data, whether or not an alleged consequence of the theory is indeed implied by the latter. For unless this requirement is fulfilled, the theory has no definite content, and questions as to what the theory asserts cannot be settled except by recourse to some privileged authority or arbitrary caprice. In the second place, even though the theoretical notions are not explicitly defined by way of overt empirical procedures and observable traits of things, nevertheless at least *some* theoretical notions must be *tied down* to *fairly definite and unambiguously specified* observable materials, by way of rules of procedure variously called 'correspondence rules,' 'coordinating definitions,' and 'operational definitions.' For if this condition is not satisfied, the theory can have no determinate consequences about *empirical* subject matter. An immediate corollary to these requirements is that since a consistent theory cannot imply two incompatible consequences, a credible theory must not only be *confirmed* by observational evidence, but it must also be capable of being *negated* by such evidence. In short, a theory must not be formulated in such a manner that it can always be construed and manipulated so as to explain whatever the actual facts are, no matter whether controlled observation shows one state of affairs to obtain or its opposite." (19, pp. 39–40.)

Lindzey and Nagel both use the helpful terminology developed by philosophers. For the present discussion, I would like to use "theoretical language" and "observational language" from Carnap (see page 9 above) to refer to the distinctions they make.

In Carnap's terminology the difficulties with Freudian theory reduce particularly to these two: it is hard to find clear and consistent definitions of its theoretical terms, and the theoretical terms are not clearly linked to behavior-level terms by means of an observational language. It is toward the resolution of these difficulties that the following discussion is aimed.

IX

✗ The Theoretical Language of Repression and Defense

THE first question is whether Freud's theory can be expressed clearly and consistently at the abstract level. The present chapter is an effort to achieve a logical presentation of the main ideas of the theory. It must be emphasized that the outline presented here depends for its full meaning on the comprehensive statement of Freud's theory in Part One; before proceeding the reader may wish to review the summaries for Chapters I–VIII.

I. *"Defense" refers to a variety of effects that arise out of the interplay of forces on psychological processes.*

    A. These variable effects have the theoretical status of alternative manifestations of defense, which is conceived, on the most abstract level, as one general type of process.

    B. The alternative manifestations of the one general process appear, on the observational level, as the different particular defenses.

    C. "Repression" is a term that Freud employed inconsistently but it has, nevertheless, a clear and consistent reference to his underlying concepts. Its conceptual reference is to certain individual defenses, to certain subgroups of defenses, and to defensive manifestations in therapy.

    D. On the most abstract level, "repression" has the same conceptual structure as "defense" but is more limited in that it refers only to *certain* effects of the interplay of forces, while "defense" refers to *all* such effects.

142

E. The effects of repression like those of defense are variable and appear as alternative manifestations of the one general process.

F. In Freud's use "repression" had as its principal references four conceptually distinguishable types of effect upon psychological processes.

   1. Effects on the conscious representation of instinctual drives and material associated with them.

     a. Unconsciously motivated forgetting (amnesic repression).

     b. Repressive defenses.

   2. Inhibitory effects upon emotions and activities.

     a. Emotional inhibition.

     b. Ego-restriction, or behavioral inhibition.

   3. Certain effects on consciousness, emotions, and behavior in therapy which, together, were called resistances.

   4. Certain responses to the interplay of force and counterforce that take place in infancy and childhood (primal repression).

G. Thus, the concepts of repression and defense overlap completely along most of their extent. "Repression" covers the main bulk of the defenses. Its scope includes all that "defense" covers except for the few remaining reactions of regression, sublimation, condemnation, and absorption. There is not, in Freud, a theory of defense and a separate theory of repression; there is rather one concept of a force and counterforce interacting, with this interplay manifesting itself in a wide variety of alternative forms. Defense refers to *all* these forms, and repression, in Freud's theory, refers to *nearly* all. The most accurate terminology is, then, "Freud's theory of repression *and* defense."

II. *The force and counterforce in repression and defense are instinctual drives and anticathexes.*

A. The instinctual forces.

   1. The instinctual forces involved in repression and defense are either "primal motives" or motives that have associative connections with such primal motives.

     a. Primal motives are motives which Freud considered to be expressions of childhood sexuality. They are of two types:

       (1) Pregenital drives (oral, anal, or phallic).

       (2) Oedipal impulses — the incestual wishes toward parents.

143

        b. Associated motives are motives having associative connections to the primal motives.

           (1) Childhood associated pregenital motives have origins independent of the pregenital drives (oral, anal, phallic), but very soon, and invariably, become closely linked with them.

           (2) Adult associated motives, like adult (or genital) sex and adult hostility, are repressible only if associatively connected with repressed primal motives.

  2. The instinctual forces involved in repression have somatic origins. They are self-energizing, in contrast to motives that are aroused by external stimulation, and they act as constant forces that strive uninterruptedly toward discharge.

        a. The instinctual forces constantly strive for expression in behavior and consciousness.

        b. They are normally represented in consciousness by ideas and feelings (affects).

        c. When not repressed, these idea-affect representations of instinct are naturally conscious.

B. The anti-instinctual or anticathectic forces.

  1. "Anticathexis" refers to a force having certain properties.

        a. It has a certain degree of strength.

        b. It has a definite psychological direction in that it is *opposed* to the direction that instincts have.

        c. It is a constant force, exerting an *uninterrupted* counter-instinct pressure.

        d. It is unconscious because of its associative connections with repressed primal motives.

  2. Anticathexis is not an independent motivational force. Its existence depends upon anxiety as the ultimate motive for repression. Anxiety has two general forms:

        a. Traumatic anxiety.

           (1) Traumatic anxiety is a state of overwhelming psychic helplessness.

           (2) It may also be described as a state of overtension caused by the flooding of the organism with stimulation beyond its capacity to control.

           (3) Anxiety of a traumatic intensity occurs in three kinds

of human experience, only the last of which is important in the theory of repression and defense:

(a) War situations.

(b) Adult sexual excitement that is ungratified.

(c) In childhood, when the organism's capacity to protect itself against such excessive stimulation is weak.

(4) Childhood or primal traumas have three general origins:

(a) They occur in infancy when physiological needs are not gratified.

(b) In early childhood, separation from the mother can be a traumatic experience.

(c) In later childhood, the threat of castration is a universal human trauma.

b. Signal anxiety fundamentally is an anticipatory fear experienced by the adult that the primal traumas of childhood, which are now unconscious (since they are repressed), will recur if adult impulses having associative connections with primal motives are acted upon.

3. When the anticathectic force is at work in the therapeutic situation, it is called "resistance." "Resistance" may refer either to the hypothetical anticathectic force or to the observable behavior from which the existence of the force is inferred.

a. Resistance shows certain characteristics:

(1) It is unconscious.

(2) It is of variable strength at different stages of therapy.

b. There are five types of resistance, the first three of which are forms of ego-resistance:

(1) Repression-resistance. This centers around the patient's difficulties in following the requirement to tell everything in free association, but includes almost anything that delays change in the patient. Blocking in associations and changing the wording of dreams on second telling are examples on a behavioral level.

(2) Transference resistance. The patient's development of feelings of hostility or of sexual love toward the therapist was interpreted by Freud as an attempt to avoid

145

remembering what he was afraid to tell. Affectionate feelings toward the therapist are not a form of resistance.

(3) Resistance from the gain of illness. The patient is unwilling to give up the secondary advantages that he has gained from being ill and resists cure for this reason.

(4) Resistance of the unconscious and resistance from a sense of guilt. These are non-ego forms of resistance. Both have in common a "need to suffer."

    (a) Resistance from a sense of guilt. The person's severe superego makes it necessary that he should remain ill as punishment, so he resists cure.

    (b) Resistance of the unconscious. Certain tendencies of the id result in this form of resistance:

        (i) The innate tendency to repeat actions of the past.

        (ii) The tendency of unconscious processes in the id to draw conscious material into the unconscious like a magnet.

        (iii) A loss of psychic plasticity, an exhaustion of the capacity for change.

III. *The interaction of instinctual and anticathectic forces results in two types of outcome: the attempt at repression and defense is either successful or unsuccessful.*

A. Successful defense. The anticathectic force aims to do away with the instinctual force. When the instinctual force is eliminated in such a way that it loses its original character as an unacceptable primal motive the anticathectic effort is successful. Freud spoke of these successful outcomes in various terms, at times calling them successful defenses; some were referred to in a very general way as successful repressions, at least one was specifically called repression, and some were sharply distinguished from repression. If one uses an exact language that follows Freud's underlying concepts rather than his actual word usage, the responses considered in this section would never be called repressions, since repression only disguises or inhibits unacceptable motives, whereas all the reactions to be considered herein involve actually altering or destroying the unacceptable impulse. Technically, then, these are best thought of as successful *defenses*, even though, when speaking loosely, Freud often referred to them as successful repressions. Successful defenses are characteristic of normalcy as contrasted to the unsuccessful defense of pathology, though normal persons also use some unsuccessful defenses.

1. Sublimation.
   a. At times Freud definitely distinguished sublimation as being different from repression. It would most correctly be called a successful defense, both by Freud's principal usages and by the logic of his theory.
   b. It is used as a defense against pregenital impulses, particularly oral and anal.
   c. Sublimation involves drive substitution in which an unacceptable pregenital drive is replaced by a socially acceptable one. Artistic activity replacing pregenital drives was Freud's principal example.
   d. The pregenital drives involved become "desexualized." Desexualization is a change in which a motive loses its sexual quality and becomes motivationally neutral.
   e. Sublimation can only deal with limited amounts of pregenital sexual motivation and many persons possess only a slight capacity for sublimation.
2. Destruction in the id.
   a. Freud spoke of this as a form of repression while also distinguishing it sharply from repression.
   b. It is not clear whether destruction in the id is to be regarded as a separate defense or as the outcome of the action of various other defenses on the impulses of the Oedipus complex.
   c. Freud applied "destruction in the id" to the incestual wishes of the Oedipus complex and said that in normal development the Oedipus complex was "destroyed."
   d. "Destruction" implies a complete elimination of the instinctual force.
3. Absorption.
   a. Freud explicitly distinguished absorption from sublimation and repression.

147

      b. Absorption, like sublimation, seems to apply principally to pregenital motives.

      c. Also like sublimation it involves the replacement of unacceptable motives with socially acceptable ones. Freud gave the example of anal motives being replaced by thriftiness, orderliness, and cleanliness.

      d. The relation of absorption to sublimation and other successful defenses is not clear.

  4. Repudiation or condemnation.

      a. Freud used these two terms alternately and sharply distinguished this reaction from repression.

      b. The terms were used by Freud particularly to describe the response of patients in therapy. When the analyst makes an objectionable impulse conscious through his interpretations, the healthy response is to examine it and condemn it on the basis of judgment. The effect is to leave a conscious memory of the impulses but the motivational charge itself is destroyed. While Freud applied this concept to cases in therapy, there is an implication that this is also a normal response outside of therapy.

B. Unsuccessful defense. The anticathectic force in unsuccessful defense does not succeed in actually changing the objectionable character of the impulse, but only in forcing a disguise, an inhibition, or a retreat to another impulse, one that appeared earlier developmentally but is also objectionable. All but a very tiny fraction of Freud's writings on repression and defense are about unsuccessful defense. In fact the terms "repression" and "defense" when used without qualification in Freud's writings automatically refer to unsuccessful repression and defense.

  1. Repressive defenses. The concept of defense was first formulated by Freud in terms of the effects of certain ways of responding to the interplay of instinct versus anticathectic force — responding by means of various alterations in the conscious representation of the instinct involved. Freud specifically called each of a large number of such consciousness-altering responses "a form of repression." His formal definition of "repression" was made in terms of the effects of the response on the conscious representation of instinct. Herein it was sug-

gested that Freud had a definite concept in his thinking which he never named, but which, once recognized, introduces order into his otherwise confusing terminology. It was proposed that the whole group of reactions that achieve ego-protection against instincts chiefly by using a consciousness-altering defense mechanism be called "repressive defenses."

a. Amnesic repression. The first-described repressive defense was amnesia, or unconsciously motivated forgetting as a defense against instincts. Freud never varied in his usage of "repression" as a specific name for amnesia, despite his many other changing uses for the word. Because of its special historical role, the long-established and consistent usage by both psychoanalysts and experimental psychologists, and the fact that its effects on consciousness are somewhat different from those of other repressive defenses, it is necessary to give amnesic repression a separate designation within the category of repressive defenses.

b. Other repressive defenses. This large group of defenses all differ from amnesic repression in that they achieve ego-protection through some form of *distortion* of conscious representation of impulse, while in amnesia, mental content associated with the impulse is *absent* from consciousness because it has been forgotten.

   (1) In conversion the instinctual impulse is represented in consciousness in the form of a physical complaint.

   (2) Reaction-formation represents the impulse in consciousness in its opposite form.

   (3) Projection misrepresents the ownership of the impulse.

   (4) In isolation the ideational part of the impulse is present in consciousness but is separated from other ideas and from its emotional charge.

   (5) In undoing, the evil impulse is allowed expression if it is followed by an action of atonement that cancels the effects of the impulse.

   (6) In displacement the impulse is in consciousness but it is directed toward a substitute object.

   (7) Reversal seems to apply specifically to the emotion of love being changed to hate, or an active sexual impulse

149

changed to its opposite of passivity. Its difference from reaction-formation is unclear. Freud seemed to consider it to be a defense used in early childhood, while reaction-formation came later.

(8) Denial is the withdrawal of attention from a perception that has taken place and the emphasizing of a substitute.

2. Regression.

a. Regression was always distinguished sharply from repression by Freud.

b. Freud distinguished two types of regression:
 (1) Object regression.
 (2) Drive regression.

c. Regression involves a substitution of childhood sexual objects (parents) or pregenital drives for mature heterosexual objects or genital drives.

d. The substitution involves a developmental dimension in the person's life history. It is a retreat from a later to an earlier developmental stage.

e. In regression there must be a *fixation* of object or drive at the earlier developmental levels.

f. The objects or drives to which the defensive retreat is made are unacceptable, being either incestuous or pregenital. This unacceptability of the regressed object or drive necessitates the further use of repressive defenses against the substituted drives as a means of ego-protection.

g. The conscious representation of impulse is affected by the use of regression as a defense, but, unlike the repressive defenses, this alteration of consciousness is a by-product of regression rather than the main ego-protective mechanism.

3. Inhibitory defenses. In these two defenses ego-protection is achieved by inhibiting either activities that would arouse dangerous impulses or the inner development of impulses.

a. Ego-restriction or behavioral inhibition.

(1) In 1915 when Freud pointed out that one effect of repression was to prevent the development of motility and the setting off of muscular activity, this defense seemed to be a part of repression. Later he seemed to

consider it different from repression, but this is not clear.

    (2) Ego-restriction is an inhibition of activities which, if engaged in, would result in the arousal of feared impulses.

  b. Emotional inhibition.

    (1) This was first distinguished as an aspect of repression and never given a separate name.

    (2) Inhibition differs most clearly from repressive defenses. In the latter the objectionable impulse is present in consciousness but in a disguised form, while in inhibition the arousal of the impulse itself is blocked.

IV. *Repression and defense have a childhood and an adult form, with adult repression and defense causally related to the use of unsuccessful repression and defense in childhood.*

A. Childhood repression and defense.

  1. Freud called childhood repression "primal repression." By "repression" here he clearly meant the term in its general sense of "defense."

  2. Primal repression appears to cover the period from infancy up to the point when the superego has been formed.

  3. Primal repression has a different motivational basis from adult repression in that it is an automatic and instinctive response to a state of overtension resulting from unbearable amounts of stimulation. These are trauma states and the traumatic anxiety expressed in such a state is described as a feeling of overwhelming helplessness.

  4. The primal traumas that lead to primal repression are particularly non-gratification of physical needs in infancy and separation from the mother and castration threat in later childhood.

  5. The outcomes of primal repression may be successful, leading to normal development, or unsuccessful, leading to pathology.

B. Adult repression and defense.

  1. When Freud was using a more exact language than usual, adult repression was referred to variously as "repression proper," "after-pressure," or "after-expulsion." Ordinarily, he simply used "repression" to mean adult repression.

151

      2. Adult repression begins after the superego is formed (ages 5–6).

      3. It is based upon the signal-anxiety mechanism, which is an anticipatory response that warns the adult that a great danger threatens. The threatening danger is the unconscious fear that the primal traumas of childhood will recur if adult sexual or aggressive activities are engaged in which have associative connections with primal traumas.

      4. Thus, adult repression is causally connected with childhood repression. Adults can repress only insofar as they have had childhood histories of unsuccessful primal repression.

V. *Repression and defense have varying effects upon consciousness.*

    A. The repression theory centers around consciousness as the basic datum and the problem with which the theory is concerned.

    B. It is an implicit assumption in Freud's theory that the psychological processes which are subject to repression would normally be conscious except for the fact that repression has prevented this.

    C. Repressed material is absent from consciousness in certain cases.

      1. In amnesic repression — since the material is forgotten.

      2. In emotional inhibition — since the dangerous impulse has been prevented from developing by direct inhibition of it.

      3. In ego-restriction — since the dangerous impulse is not aroused: the person curtails activities that would instigate the motive.

      4. In regression — since the impulse has been replaced by a substitute. However, the substitute *is* present in consciousness in the form of a repressive-defense response.

      5. In most cases of successful repression, including sublimation, destruction in the id, and absorption.

    D. Repressed material can be present in consciousness in varying forms and states:

      1. In distorted form.

        a. As a symptom.

        b. As a repressive defense response (conversion, projection, reaction-formation, etc.).

      2. Under remote conditions when ego-recognition of the impulse and its ownership is prevented.

        a. In dreams.

152

  b. Free association.

  c. Hypnosis.

  d. Daytime fantasies.

  e. Jokes, wit, and humor.

3. In the case of the successful defense of condemnation or repudiation when the ideas involved become conscious but lose their motivational power.

X

✗ The Observational Language of Repression and Defense

THE question we turn to now is whether the "correspondence rules," "coordinating definitions," or "operational definitions" of the theoretical terms can be stated in observational language.

It may be helpful first to use an analogy with concepts and measurement in physical science. Temperature serves as a convenient comparison in the following chart:

Temperature	*Repression and Defense*

I. Theoretical Language

Temperature is a manifestation of the energy of atomic vibrations in solids and of the speed of random molecular motion in liquids and gases.	Repression and defense are manifestations of the interplay of the force of instincts and the counterforce of anti-cathexis in psychic life.

II. Observational Language

A. TYPES OF INDICATORS

1. Psychological sensations of heat and cold upon touching objects.	1. Sensations such as heartpounding, dizziness, feelings of apprehension, and similar neurotic symptoms.
2. Changes in the color of heated metals.	2. Changed extent of expression of impulse with increased remoteness (in dreams, hypnosis, fantasy, free association, joking).
3. The presence of changes in electrical resistance.	3. The presence of repressive defenses.
4. The presence of changes in pressure of gases kept at a constant volume.	4. The presence of inhibitions of feeling and behavior.
5. The presence of volumetric expansion of solids and liquids. Etc.	5. The presence of resistance in therapy.

154

Temperature	*Repression and Defense*

B. SPECIFIC TECHNIQUES FOR QUANTIFICATION OF
THE PARTICULAR INDICATOR

EXAMPLE: Volumetric expansion of liquids

1. Expansion of alcohol in a glass tube.
   a. The range of expansion is arbitrarily set as the range between the freezing and boiling points of water, with arbitrary division into 100 equal intervals (Centigrade scale).
   b. The number of units of change on the 100-interval scale is the measure.
2. Expansion of mercury in a glass tube. (Same technique.)

EXAMPLE: Resistance behavior in therapy

1. Periods of silence in free association.
   a. A 50-minute therapy period is taken as the arbitrary range of time, yielding 50 equal intervals of one minute each.
   b. The number of units out of 50 spent in silence is the measure.
2. Changes in the wording of a dream on second telling.
   a. The patient is asked to tell all dreams twice.
   b. The number of words altered on second telling is the measure of resistance.

As Nagel and others have pointed out (see the quotation, pages 139–40), psychoanalytic theory — in this case specifically Freud's theory of repression and defense — is like theories in physics in that many of the basic theoretical terms do not refer to anything directly observable. The "atomic vibrations" in solids and the "kinetic energy of random molecular motive" in liquids and gases are not directly observable. They are "inferred hypotheses," or, in everyday language, imaginative guesses as to what is happening. The fact that in the physics of heat these guesses have been convincingly established by enormous amounts of indirect evidence makes physics a very advanced science compared to psychoanalysis, with its relative lack of such indirect evidence in support of the concept of repression, but this does not alter the similarity of "heat" and "repression" as inferred constructions of the scientist's imagination.

The analogy also demonstrates the usefulness and need of distinguishing two levels of the observational language: the type of indicator, and the particular technique for measuring the indicator.

These two levels — type and technique — will be referred to throughout this chapter.

It should be noticed, first, that in measuring temperature, there are many *types of manifestation* of the unobservable phenomenon of heat energy, five of which are indicated in the analogy. Volumetric expansion of liquids is quite different from the optical color of hot metal, though both

155

are indicators of heat. Secondly, these types are not equally good indicators for a given range of heat. Liquid expansion is far more accurate than color, but, on the other hand, color is more useful for extremely high temperatures. Still more importantly, the different types of indicator do not give exactly the same results.

Even within a given type of indicator, such as the expansion of liquids, alternative techniques are available. One can use mercury or alcohol in a thermometer. They do *not* give *exactly* the same reading. It should be noted too that the range of expansion used, between the freezing and boiling points of water, is arbitrarily chosen. And within this range the intervals can be Centigrade or Fahrenheit.

Considered against the background of this analysis of temperature and its observational language, Freud's theory of repression does not seem so inconsistent or so difficult to translate into the framework of science. When he says that symptoms, repressive defenses, inhibitions, the remote expressions of impulse or resistance are all "forms of repression," this is not inconsistency, but a reflection of the fact that the repression tendency has a variety of manifestations, as does heat energy.

This chapter will explore the possibility of expressing these various alternative manifestations of repression and defense in an observational language.

RESISTANCE AS AN INDICATOR OF REPRESSION

The phenomenon of resistance in therapy, with which the theory of repression began, is the easiest of the types of indicators to translate into an observational language. This is fortunate, since it is the main cornerstone of the theory on the abstract level. It also lends itself most easily to observational formulation on the level of technique.

As we saw in Chapter IV, resistance is not a homogeneous indicator; there are five subtypes: repression-resistance, transference resistance, resistance from secondary gain of illness, resistance of the unconscious, and resistance from a sense of guilt.

Indicators of Repression-Resistance. Since the concept of repression-resistance is closely related to the person's response to the fundamental rule of therapy to tell everything that comes to mind, most of the observable behaviors Freud pointed to as signs of such resistance are in the nature of failures to follow the fundamental rule. References to specific types of these failures are numerous in Freud's writings. There is no problem here of knowing what one should try to observe. The behaviors in the following partial list are all taken directly from Freud; many others could be added.

1. Periods of silence.

2. Verbal complaints to the analyst that (a) nothing comes to mind; (b) too much comes to mind to be able to speak of everything; (c) what comes to mind is too unimportant to mention; (d) what comes to mind is too absurd to mention; (e) what comes to mind is about some other person and should be exempt from the rule.

3. The keeping back of conscious material about which the patient decides to make a mental reservation and to exclude from therapy because of its special nature. Such reservations are revealed at a later time in therapy.

4. Absurd associations.

5. Circuitous associations.

6. Manifest intellectual opposition to the theory of psychoanalysis.

7. Manifest interest in being instructed by the therapist in the theory of psychoanalysis.

8. A hidden, unexpressed reservation about the validity of the theory of psychoanalysis which is not revealed until much time has passed.

9. Manifest expressions of doubt as to whether a particular detail of remembered past events, or of a remembered dream, is correct.

10. The altering, on second telling, of particular details in relating past happenings or dreams.

11. Failures to remember details of past events, or of dreams, as evidenced by their later recall in therapy.

12. Vagueness of memory in relating past history or dreams.

13. The seizing upon of accidental interruptions to therapy and exaggerating them in such a way as to delay therapy.

14. Inability to associate about certain topics suggested by the analyst.

15. Repetitious associations centering monotonously upon one topic.

For most of these, techniques could easily be developed that would give rough quantitative estimates of the indicator. The following are some examples by way of suggestion.

1. A Repression-Resistance Ratio. Since many of the behaviors listed are simply alternate ways of expressing resistance and, in this sense, are equivalent to one another, one technique might seek to assess their over-all power. With verbatim recordings (including, of course, timed periods

157

of silence) made under standard instructions, and with standardized time periods (30 or 50 minutes, for example), one could treat the total time period of the therapy hour as a unit and ask what proportion of it was occupied by behavior classifiable as resistance. This would yield a simple ratio (.20, .75, etc.) easily used in quantitative comparisons.

The development of such a measure would involve several steps:

a. Really extensive study of Freud to collect all possible examples that he specifically labeled as resistance behavior of the "repression-resistance" type. The limited material presented in this book would not suffice for this purpose.

b. Reduction of these examples by experts to a workable grouping of types of resistance behavior. A number of the clearest examples could be retained as illustrations of each type.

c. The collection of a large number of contemporary examples from verbatim records of today's best therapists.

d. Classification of these new examples by experts, using comparative judgment, as equivalent to one or another of Freud's types.

e. Addition of the contemporary examples to those defining examples from Freud in (b) above.

f. Proof that research workers (other than the experts employed in the development of the procedure) could reliably use the resulting classificatory scheme.

2. A Resistance Check List. One would not want to depend solely on a time ratio. It might be that some types of resistance behavior are more important than others. A single occurrence, for instance, might be very important even when a "resistance ratio" based on time units shows little resistance behavior. Freud points out such a possibility in the case of the patient who has a concealed doubt about the validity of the whole procedure — this intellectual resistance permits him to show all the manifest signs of cooperation but the procedure does not affect him emotionally.

A first step in identifying such uniquely important resistances would be to use a simple check list in which occurrence or nonoccurrence of a particular class of resistance behavior, and frequency of occurrence, would be tabulated over the whole period of therapy.

3. Silence Ratio. It is obvious that one could devise a ratio that would be an index of the proportion of the standard therapy hour spent in silence.

4. Thematic Rigidity Index. The concern with an unvarying theme, as in the case of Dora who spent all her initial therapy hours complaining

monotonously about her father, could be easily measured by an index of the proportion of the therapy hour spent on one theme. Counting the number of themes brought up during the hour would get at the same problem.

5. Index of Deviation from Suggested Association Topics. Freud said he found it hard to get Dora to talk about Herr K. One could devise a procedure in which the therapist would suggest associative topics that he felt the person was particularly resistive about and then observe the length of time the patient persisted with the suggested topic. This would be an easy technique to repeat for comparative purposes.

6. Index of Changes of Detail on Repetition. If dreams are reported, it would be easy to introduce a standard procedure of asking the patient to repeat his description of the dream a second time, and later comparing changes in the recorded transcript. Similarly the patient's account of significant events in his history could be used.

Indicators of Transference Resistance. Just as repression-resistances center around various forms of transgression of the fundamental rule of therapy to speak all that comes to mind, so transference resistance centers around one main aspect of therapy — in this case, the patient's emotional attitudes toward the therapist. These would seem to be easily observable.

There are two particular problems in the development of estimates of transference resistance. One is that Freud's writings seem to provide relatively few concrete examples of what patients actually said or did that indicated transference resistance. The general type of material to be observed is clear enough: negative attitudes toward the therapist on the one hand and declarations of passionate love for the analyst by women. In addition, in the case of male patients with male therapists, Freud indicated that attitudes of personal and intellectual independence, and strivings to outdo the therapist (ambition) were types of transference resistance. But what actual statements by the patient would be instances of these types of behavior? The experts would have to do more guessing here than in the case of repression-resistance, where specific examples are plentiful.

The second problem concerns positive transference. The case of negative transference seems clear — *all* negative attitudes are countable as resistance. But with positive transference, one has to distinguish between "affectionate or friendly" feelings for the therapist, which are not transference resistance, and passionate love, which is. The extremes are easy enough but a problem might arise on the borderland between the two.

159

If we turn to technique, several ingenious new methods already in use seem ready-made for the task of measurement.

1.The Q Sort and the Adjective Check List. These methods are similar in conception and application. It might be wise to experiment with both until one or the other shows its superiority for this problem. Perhaps, each would find a use in observation of different aspects of transference. They have high efficiency. The Q technique, espoused especially by Stephenson (22), is quite simply explained by Mowrer (18, pp. 316–75); a useful form of the adjective check list (ACL) has been developed by Gough and Suczek (10).

Basically the Q sort and adjective check list are ways of describing another person (or oneself). Instead of simply asking the patient to describe the therapist, for instance, and leaving him free to choose his own words, one provides him with a ready-made list of adjectives (in the ACL technique) or short descriptive phrases (in the Q-sort technique) which he checks or sorts as being in his opinion characteristic or not characteristic of the therapist. Both allow easy use of efficient quantitative comparisons; with the Q sort one can even calculate correlation coefficients to determine how similar a given characterization is to another. This technique could be used before, during, and after a period of transference resistance.

The key problem with both techniques lies in the choice of adjectives or phrases to constitute the population of items for the patient to use in describing the therapist. Approximately a hundred items are found in the usual Q-sort decks and several hundred in the ACL procedure, where the patient's task is easier and he can therefore cover more items in an hour's testing time. These items would have to be ones that psychoanalytic experts would consider suitable as "transference language." Their selection would involve a considerable research problem in itself.

2. A Transference Distortion Ratio. Since transference attitudes are "unreal" in that they do not derive from the actual character and behavior of the analyst, it might be fruitful to try to observe how much of a distortion of reality is present. This would require an estimate of the real characteristics of the analyst, which could be compared with the distorted appraisal of the patient. The ACL and Q-sort procedures could be used for both. A "real" estimate of the therapist could be derived from one-way screen observations of the therapist in action made by experts, who would then use ACL or Q-sort items to describe the analyst's personality in

the therapy room. Items on which the experts agree would constitute the "real" estimate. With the Q sort one could then correlate the patient's estimate with "reality" and express the degree of distortion in correlational terms.

Of course it is possible to use the same correlational method to investigate the extent to which the attributes of some other particular person are being imputed to the analyst. Since, according to Freud, the emotional attitudes are "transferred" from early relationships to parents and other significant figures, it might be fruitful to correlate the patient's Q-sort description of his father, for example, with his Q-sort description of the analyst. Presumably, in the case of a "father transference" the correlation would increase as the transference resistance became more intense.

Resistance Due to Secondary Gain of Illness. While the general nature of the concept of secondary gain seems reasonably clear it does not, on first study at least, readily suggest many possible observational procedures.

Resistance from a Sense of Guilt. This type of resistance seems accessible to observation through procedures aimed at estimating feelings of guilt and self-punitive attitudes.

1. Guilt feelings. Since the guilt is unconscious, one could not employ measures which directly ask the patient whether he feels guilty. Experts would have to select from verbatim therapy protocols examples of responses from the patient that represent instances of "unconscious guilt." If consensus between independent experts is demonstrable, the best of these responses could be assembled into a population of Q-sort sentences and phrases and the patient asked to sort them according to how true he believes them to be ("Fate is hard, but we deserve every bit of what we get in life"), or the extent to which they characterize him ("I never complain about my hard lot in life").

2. Superego strictness.

a. Discrepancies between Self-Ideal and Self. Freud's formulation of the superego as having the functions of self-observation, of holding up ideals, and of criticizing the failures of the ego in attaining these, offers fruitful possibilities in development of techniques that are already being widely exploited.

Gough and Suczek (10, p. 15) describe such a technique employed by Leary, Bronson, Wanda, and Harvey. Patients were first asked to characterize their personalities as they actually were, using the adjective check list. Next, they were asked to complete the check list a second time, giving

161

a description of the "ideal self" (how one would like to be). Their study showed a discrepancy index between self and ideal self of 74 for forty neurotic patients, 52 for fourteen ulcer patients, and 44 for twenty-six hypertension cases.

Rogers and his co-workers have employed Q sorts about self and ideal self for the same purpose in their studies of therapeutic processes (20). Correlations between ideal self and self for normal controls before and after therapy were .58 and .59, while patients moved from a —.01 (no correlation!) between self and ideal self to a correlation of .31. The changes that took place in the patients were in the nature of a lowering of impossibly high ideals — entirely in line with a Freudian prediction.

Neither the Gough check list items nor the Rogerian Q-sort items were selected on the basis of any explicit theory, though the Rogerian picture of personality undoubtedly served as an implicit guide to their item selection. If one were working with Freudian theory, the items would be selected from verbatim protocols (with modifications to make them suitable as test items, but retaining their essence) according to the judgment of Freudian experts.

b. Self-criticality. The Freudian theory in a general sense probably gave rise to Gough and Suczek's ingenious suggestion of measuring self-punitiveness through a self-criticality ratio (10, p. 15). Each of the 300 words in their adjective check list was rated by a sample of judges for "favorability" and "unfavorability." The 75 most and least favorable adjectives were used to calculate a ratio of the number of favorable to unfavorable self-descriptive adjectives used. The higher the proportion of unfavorable adjectives checked, the more self-critical the person (and presumably the more severe his superego). Since a person filling out the ACL would not be aware that he was checking more favorable or more unfavorable items, the procedure seems to be one that could get at unconscious self-punitive tendencies.

Again, one would want to select adjectives or phrases from therapy material by using judges working consciously in the Freudian framework.

c. Strictness of attitudes toward childhood prohibitions. Since the superego is a precipitate of the childhood period and continues the injunctions of parents, it would be especially appropriate to use measures that tap the person's attitudes toward childhood problems. In Mark's study (17), for instance, mothers of schizophrenics were asked to fill out a questionnaire having to do with how people should rear their children. Some typical items were these:

"Children should be taken to and from school until the age of eight just to make sure there are no accidents."

"Most children are toilet trained by 15 months of age."

"Children who take part in sex play become sex criminals when they grow up."

"It is all right for a mother to sleep with a child because it gives him a feeling of being loved and wanted."

Hanfmann and Getzels (11) present suggestive evidence that asking a person to fill out such indirect questionnaires — rather than asking directly "What do you think?" — gets at more unconscious material.

Again, of course, the items used would have to be chosen for their theoretical relevance.

Resistance of the Unconscious. This concept seems too unclear in Freud's own writings to suggest observational possibilities. It is hard to distinguish this second form of a "need to be ill" from resistance due to a sense of guilt. At one point Freud refers to suicidal tendency as a concrete expression of the concept. Rating scales directed at estimating suicidal tendency would presumably be a suitable technique in this case. Freud also makes this form of resistance "responsible for working through" and attributes this necessity for "working through" to the repetition-compulsion tendency. Presumably, measures aimed at estimating how often patients returned to the therapist with the same problems in a new form after earlier instances of the same tendency had been interpreted and corrected would furnish estimates of such repetition tendency.

REPRESSIVE DEFENSE AS AN INDICATOR OF REPRESSION

A repressive defense is, basically, a general indicator of repression tendency. Instances at the behavioral level of any one of the repressive defenses would be the observation data for this general type of indicator.

Among the repressive defenses Freud included the particular mechanisms of amnesia, conversion, isolation, undoing, projection, displacement, reaction-formation, and denial (including negation). All these response patterns serve the general purpose of ego-protection against anxiety-arousing impulses. They all protect the person from the threat of an impulse by creating unawareness toward some aspect of the response pattern. This unawareness enables the person to avoid fully acknowl-

163

edging the impulse as belonging to himself. This does not mean that all the patterns have equal clinical significance in their implication for the patient's therapeutic accessibility, or his prognosis, but they are all equivalent as controls of awareness that make up one main type of repression. Of course, insofar as each type of repressive defense has different prognostic significance, one would want to retain their separate identity for some purposes, even though all are forms of repression in the theory.

In technique, one would want to develop an acceptable series of rating scales as the means of estimating the extent to which each of the repressive defenses was present in a given case. Here are the steps that might be involved:

1. A search of Freud's writings for two kinds of material relating to each repressive defense.* One would first need a general theoretical statement of the qualitative nature of the response pattern in question. Conversion might serve as an example. A series of abstract definitional statements about conversion would be taken verbatim from Freud's works. For example: "In hysteria the unbearable idea is rendered innocuous by the quantity of excitation attached to it being transmuted into some bodily form of expression, a process for which I should like to propose the name of *conversion*" (1894, p. 63); ". . . in hysteria the repression is effectively established by means of *conversion* into bodily innervation . . ." (1896, p. 169); ". . . the translation of a purely psychical excitation into physical terms — the process which I have called 'conversion' . . ." (1905b, p. 53). Such defining statements taken together would constitute the conceptual part of Freud's meaning of "conversion."

The same procedure should eventually be followed with theorists who came after Freud before a final conception is settled on.

To establish the observation-level correlates of the concept of conversion the same type of search would be made for a large number of actual clinical illustrations in which Freud (and others) described conversion behavior. One example can be taken from the Dora case:

"Dora had had a very large number of attacks of coughing accompanied by loss of voice. Could it be that the presence or absence of the man she loved had had an influence upon the appearance and disappearance of the symptom of her illness? If this were so, it must be possible to dis-

* The account of each individual defense presented in this book would not be sufficient for this purpose.

cover some coincidence or other which would betray the fact. I asked her what the average length of these attacks had been. 'From three to six weeks, perhaps.' How long had Herr K.'s absence lasted? 'Three to six weeks, too,' she was obliged to admit. Her illness was therefore a demonstration of her love for Herr K. . . .

"So it is not to be wondered at that this hysterical girl of nearly nineteen, who had heard of the occurrence of such a method of sexual intercourse (sucking at the male organ), should have developed an unconscious phantasy of this sort and should have given it expression by an irritation in her throat and by coughing. . . .

"The production of a symptom of this kind [Dora's cough] . . . [is] the translation of a purely psychical excitation into physical terms — [is] the process which I have called 'conversion' . . ." (1905b, pp. 39, 51, 53.)

Note that in this example of behavior it is certain that the symptoms of coughing and aphonia together with their psychological context are instances of conversion, since Freud specifically labels them at the end. All the defining examples collected should have been labeled by Freud in this way, or else one should be certain from other evidence that Freud would have labeled them "conversion."

The general defining statements and behavioral examples, from Freud and other theorists, all typed in full verbatim form, would constitute the data on which the eventual rating scale for conversion could be developed.

2. The collection of a series of modern-day theoretical definitions and observational examples of the defense in question. Since the intention would not be to confine oneself to repression "as Freud meant it," one would want to collect such material from the important theorists and clinicians since Freud. The examples would best be taken from recorded therapy protocols by the best contemporary analysts.

The most expert and experienced analysts available would have to agree on the best final definitional statement of each defense and select a series of critical examples that would define different *degrees* of the use of the defense in question. These definitions plus their degree-defining examples would constitute a rating scale for the defense.

It would then need to be shown that new independent judges could use the definitional statements and rating-scale examples to classify reliably new instances of each defense.

A "Life History Amnesia Index" could be used with indicators of repressive defense. The patient's account of himself and his problems gathered by means of some sort of standard life history interview could provide the material for such an index. Comparison of the patient's account at the beginning and end of treatment and at selected intervening points would show the amount of gain in the completeness of his story.

In the Dora case, Freud suggested that patients are unable to give complete accounts at the beginning partly because of amnesias (1905b, pp. 16–17), and that at the end of treatment the life history is much more complete, its completeness coinciding with the patient's loss of symptoms (pp. 24–25). If one had a standard sample of the patient's story at two or more points in treatment, it might be possible to work out ways of rating the extent of completeness in the history and to construct a scale of degrees of change in completeness. "It is only towards the end of treatment that we have before us an intelligible, consistent, and unbroken case history" (1905b, p. 18).

The repressive defense of reaction-formation deserves a special place as an indicator because it is a relatively pure index of the anticathectic force. The anticathectic force is an inferred construct, of course, something one does not directly perceive. But in the case of the repressive defenses of reaction-formation and denial Freud seemed to feel that the manifestation of anticathexis in behavior stood in a much more direct relation to theory than usual:

"Resistance presupposes the existence of what I have called *anticathexis*. An anticathexis of this kind is clearly seen in obsessional neurosis. It appears there in the form of an alteration of the ego, as a reaction-formation in the ego, and is effected by the reinforcement of the attitude which is the opposite of the instinctual trend that has to be repressed — as, for instance, in pity, conscientiousness and cleanliness. These reaction-formations of obsessional neurosis are essentially exaggerations of the normal traits of character which develop during the latency period. The presence of an anticathexis in hysteria is much more difficult to detect, though theoretically it is equally indispensable. In hysteria, too, a certain amount of alteration of the ego through reaction-formation is unmistakable and in some circumstances becomes so marked that it forces itself on our attention as the principal symptom. The conflict due to ambivalence, for instance, is resolved in hysteria by this means. The subject's hatred of a person whom he loves is kept down by an exaggerated amount of tenderness for him and apprehensiveness about him. But the difference between reaction-formations in obsessional neurosis and in hysteria is that in the latter they do not have the universality of a character-trait but are confined to particular relationships." (1926b, pp. 157–58.)

Reaction-formation, then, would seem to be an unusually "pure" estimate of the counterforce tendency and would be of particular theoretical interest as an estimate of repression.

If procedures such as the foregoing yielded rating scales for each separate repressive defense, one would certainly want to experiment with combining them into a pooled estimate. Any one patient typically uses a number of defenses. In the Dora case, there is not only the repressive amnesia that Freud considered distinctive of hysteria, but also displacement, reversal of affect, projection, and regression, and perhaps others. The significant measure might be one that groups together all repressive defenses into one score. This over-all estimate of repressive defense might be applied to standard interview hours taken at various points during therapy.

The repressive defense of denial is of particular interest because it seems to parallel closely what psychologists have been calling "perceptual defense" in recent studies of the perception of threatening material (1). The research methods developed in these studies over the past decade hold promise for work with repression. They have used a camera shutter arrangement or a tachistoscope to flash the word, sentence, or picture employed as a threatening stimulus — giving the subject only the briefest glimpse. If the subject delays in recognizing dangerous material as compared to neutral stimuli, perceptual denial would presumably have occurred. Thus far few of the studies have tried to employ either stimuli or subjects that the theory of repression is concerned with. Blum (2, 3) came closest when he used as stimuli the "Blackie Test" pictures, which have an assumed pregenital sexual content. Blum's subjects were graduate students, but if one used hysterical and phobic patients with pregenital and genital sexual stimuli the experimental analogue to anticathectic perceptual denial would be quite close.

Freud's own account of perceptual denial is of particular relevance here:

"What had happened, therefore, was that the boy had refused to take cognizance of the fact perceived by him that a woman had no penis. No, that cannot be true, for if a woman can be castrated then his own penis is in danger; and against that there rebels part of his narcissism which

Nature has providentially attached to this particular organ. In later life grown men may experience a similar panic, perhaps when the cry goes up that throne and altar are in danger, and similar illogical consequences will also follow then. If I am not mistaken, Laforgue would say in this case that the boy 'scotomizes' the perception of the woman's lack of a penis. Now a new term is justified when it describes a new fact or brings it into prominence. There is nothing of that kind here; the oldest word in our psychoanalytical terminology, 'repression', already refers to this pathological process. If we wish to differentiate between what happens to the *idea* as distinct from the *affect*, we can restrict 'repression' to relate to the affect; the correct use for what happens to the idea is then 'denial'. 'Scotomization' seems to me particularly unsuitable, for it suggests that the perception is promptly obliterated, so that the result is the same as when a visual impression falls on the blind spot on the retina. In the case we are discussing, on the contrary, we see that the perception has persisted and that a very energetic action has been exerted to keep up the denial of it. It is not true that the child emerges from his experience of seeing the female parts with an unchanged belief in the woman having a phallus. He retains this belief but he also gives it up; during the conflict between the deadweight of the unwelcome perception and the force of the opposite wish, a compromise is constructed such as is only possible in the realm of unconscious modes of thought — by the primary processes. In the world of psychical reality the woman still has a penis in spite of all, but this penis is no longer the same as it once was. Something else has taken its place, has been appointed its successor, so to speak, and now absorbs all the interest which formerly belonged to the penis." (1927, pp. 199–200.)

It is to be particularly noted in this quotation that once the threatening percept registered it could not be *obliterated* by the repression tendency. Rather, repression works in this case by withdrawing attention from the percept and emphasizing a substitute. This suggests that "perceptual defense" stimuli will have to be ones where it is not only possible to see the stimulus in the dangerous way, but also, just as easily, in a harmless, substitute way.

For instance, if one flashed the scrambled phrase "arm, your, break, shake" and instructed the subjects to report meaningful phrases, telling them that if they dropped out one word, the remaining three would always combine into a meaningful phrase, a situation would be established in which the dangerous percept can be denied by the harmless substitute phrase becoming accentuated in consciousness.

AFFECT INHIBITION AS AN INDICATOR OF REPRESSION

In affect inhibition the emotional experience is prevented from developing so that there is an absence of emotion in a situation where one would have expected strong feelings. Freud spoke loosely of these inhibited feelings as "unconscious emotions" or "unconscious affects," although he clearly acknowledged that, in this new case, he did not mean to imply that the emotional process *exists* in the unconscious; only a *potential* for the development of feeling remains. He did not amplify in detail what "potential" meant, saying only that in therapy the capacity for the heretofore missing emotional experience is restored so that the patient once again *has* feelings at the points where these were absent in the repressed state.

We need to introduce here a new concept: the "strength of emotional instigation" of the situation in relation to which the patient's behavior is to be judged. If we estimate the strength of emotional response in relation to the emotional instigative strength of the situation, we can have an observational-level index of repression that is very close to the theoretical formulation.

It would not be difficult for clinical judges to rate instances of emotional behavior related by the patient in the initial life history interview, or further material revealed in free association or therapy interchanges, in terms of adequacy of emotional response to instigations that the patient experienced. The patient may relate, for instance, that recently his spouse, or a colleague, insulted him in such and such a way, but that he felt indifferent and experienced no anger, even though, in the judgment of the clinical rater, there was strong provocation to anger.

During the course of therapy itself, natural occasions for anger on the part of the patient inevitably arise. The therapist blunders, he is late or misses an appointment, goes on a vacation, etc. When such incidents occur in recorded protocol material, they could be used for ratings of affect inhibition.

As another approach one could intentionally provide situations designed to instigate emotional responses. Thus, the patient might be told by the secretary upon his arrival that the therapist had not yet come in, or even phoned in, and that he should sit and wait. She could observe and

169

record his response and behavior, for some standard time period. The therapist would then "arrive" and proceed with the session without apology, and the session would be recorded and rated for adequacy of anger response.

With slightly more formalization of the situation one can create fairly controlled experimental situations for some emotions, most easily for anger. This has already been extensively experimented with in the "ego-insult" technique in psychology. Interestingly enough, although the experimental subject is typically insulted or made anxious about his intellectual adequacy, his emotional response itself is never systematically observed in these "repression" studies. Rather, the experimenter attempts to ascertain whether the subject "represses" by seeing what effect the insult or the arousal of anxiety has upon memory for words (often nonsense words) learned in the same situation in which the emotion is aroused. The present formulation of the repression theory would suggest that the emotions of the subject ought to be one of the main things observed!

Many ego-insult or anxiety-arousing techniques used today would be quite suitable for experimental instigation of emotions. One would only need to get normative data on how instigating they actually were for a suitable range of normal subjects. If a particular person then failed to develop the emotion, one could say that repressive affect inhibition was demonstrated in his case.

Several examples suggest themselves. First the observer might rate how much emotion he saw. An adjective check list or a simple rating scale would do. Next, one could arrange an informal observational situation in which the subject is asked to wait in an outer room where he finds another "subject" who has "just been through" the same procedure (actually a planted observer). The planted observer would engage the subject in casual conversation of a planned kind, which is then recorded. He would always say the same thing to each subject insofar as possible. The planted observer would start by being noncommital so that the amount of feeling spontaneously expressed by the subject can be noted; then by his comments he would express more and more feeling himself to see how easily a corresponding feeling is aroused. One would later ask the subject to rate the extent of his own feelings in the two situations.

The three techniques would furnish some interesting ways of estimating the inhibition of feeling. It is to be expected that reactions of the repressive-defense type would also arise, so that there are rich possibilities here for observing several types of repression indicators. The limitations are in the quality and range of emotion. Anger and anxiety would be easy to use, but not much else; and the degree of arousal would necessarily be mild. Nevertheless many aspects of repression might be subject to fruitful observation by such techniques, even with these limitations. The gain in control may be worth the sacrifice in limited range and quality of emotion that can be used.

In his chapter on "inhibition" in *Inhibitions, Symptoms and Anxiety*, Freud gives a detailed list of precautionary inhibitions which he groups into four general classes: sexual behavior, eating, walking, and occupational inhibitions (1926a, pp. 88–89). Measures like rating scales or check lists could be developed from these and other suggestions in his writings in the same manner as was described in detail for defenses. Examples of other techniques would include the following:

1. Eating inhibitions. One can quantify changes of emotional aversions to eating by some such device as a food aversion test. Wallen (24) and Eysenck (7, p. 105) have reported that neurotics dislike significantly more foods than normals, and that they tend to express a more intense dislike. Such tests seem ready-made devices for estimating repressive eating inhibitions.

One could also quantify changes in eating inhibition by carefully weighing the quantity of food eaten at the beginning of therapy, throughout its course, and at the end, correlating this measure with other measures of repression tendency.

2. Walking inhibitions. Estimates of actual physical distances traveled at the beginning of therapy and at various points along the way might be used as indicators of inhibition.

3. Sexual inhibitions. Situations in waiting rooms might be experimentally arranged in which seductive persons of the opposite sex would see how much interest could be aroused.

4. Work inhibitions. Depending on the nature of the patient's work, one could use such indicators as days of absence from work, tardiness, and measures of output appropriate to the job in question.

REMOTENESS AS AN INDICATOR OF REPRESSION

The theoretical notion that ordinarily repressed impulses can be in consciousness providing they are remote from the possibility of ego recognition is a fruitful idea for translation into observational language, much of which Freud clearly indicated in his writings.

Symptoms. Probably the simplest measure of repression having a perfectly clear relation to theory would be based on the presence of neurotic symptoms. Freud's writings contain a full range of examples of such symptoms and his theory that symptoms are signs of repression is perfectly clear and consistent. One has only to collect together Freud's examples of neurotic symptoms and check whether, today, clinical experts could classify material from current therapy protocols in terms that Freud used, or their modern-day equivalents, and one would have a good check-list indicator of the presence or absence of repression.

There is a special point about symptoms as repression measures in that, as "compromise-formations," they are expressions of both the force and antiforce. Strictly speaking, insofar as symptoms represent the instinctual force continued in a disguised substitute form, they are not measures of the repressive tendency but of the instinctual impulses. Hence, symptoms would seem to be less purely measures of the anticathectic force than such behaviors as resistance, reaction-formations, and inhibitions.

Situational Remoteness. To make the best use of the theoretical notion that otherwise repressed impulses can become manifest under certain conditions such as dreams, free association, fantasy, hypnosis, and joking, one has to make explicit an unstated comparison that the concept implies. If impulses are freer under free association, for instance, "freer" can only mean "freer than in non-remoteness situations." The implicit comparison is between freedom of expression of impulses under remoteness conditions as compared to freedom of such expression under more usual conditions. This comparison can be economically formulated as a ratio between direct (non-remote) and indirect (remote) expressions of impulse.

The indirect expressions of impulse are those found under remoteness conditions (dreams, free association, fantasy, hypnosis, joking). The direct expression, although implicit in Freud, is clearly meant to refer to the extent to which there is open expression of impulse in a patient's account of his life history and his daily living. It would be possible to

172

develop a series of "remoteness ratios" that are directly implied by Freud's theory. These would be ratios of directly expressed impulses to indirectly expressed impulses.

The estimate of direct expression of impulses could best be made by studying the person's detailed life history taken in some standardized way. One would have to develop ways of rating such standardized histories (as told to the therapist) for the extent impulse is expressed. Since this sort of rating has been reliably done with TAT stories by many investigators, it should offer no problem in principle, though the work involved would be considerable.

The estimate of indirect expression of impulse would be made under each of the different remoteness situations:

1. The Dream Remoteness Ratio. Freud's belief that dreams give direct access to repressed material would seem to suggest that expression of impulse through dreams as compared to direct expression would provide a fruitful ratio. And this might be so if Freud had meant that the manifest dream could indicate repressed material. Then one could have a simple ratio of extent of impulse expression in manifest dream content versus extent of impulse expression in the patient's conscious verbal picture of events in the account of his life history.

Freud believed, however, that normal and neurotic dreams are indistinguishable in manifest content. It is only by making the assumption that the manifest content is a distorted substitute for the underlying or latent content that one can use dreams as remote indicators of repressed impulses. A theoretically valid dream remoteness ratio, then, would have to be based upon the degree of impulse expression present in the *interpreted* dream versus the degree of impulse expression under less remote conditions.

In this case independent expert agreement on the interpretation of dreams, using all the Freudian assumptions of course (dream symbolism, displacement, condensation, etc.), would have to be established before one could proceed to a comparison with less remote non-dream states.

The use of *interpreted* dreams, however, would remove the dream remoteness ratio definitely from the level of observational language, since the repressed impulse is *not* observed directly in the dream but only *inferred* on the basis of further theoretical assumptions. Hence, as long as one sticks to Freud's conception of dreams, one cannot construct an observation-level indicator of the repression tendency by using dreams.

2. Free-Association Remoteness Ratio. This would be a ratio of impulse expression in a standard life history over impulse expression in a standardized and recorded free-association hour, both judged by means of suitable rating scales.

3. Hypnotic Remoteness Ratio. This would be a ratio comparing the person's life history told under waking conditions with that told under hypnotized conditions.

4. Humor Remoteness Ratio. This could best be devised by getting persons to respond to samples of impulse expression when this is open and direct as compared to the situation when impulse expression is couched in the form of humor. Possibly a series of stories or pictures depicting open and direct impulse expression could be rated by the person for degree of his liking and disliking of them, as compared to like or dislike of the impulse expression in humor.

5. Repressive-Defense Remoteness Ratio. Since, technically, repressive defenses are instances of remote expression of impulse, it would be possible to compare directly expressed impulses (life history) with defensively (repressive defenses) expressed impulses.

The Dora case might serve as an illustration here if we pretend it to be a verbatim therapy protocol. Possible instances of indirect expressions of sexual motivation in the Dora case (1905b):

1. Dora was disgusted when Herr K. kissed her at age 14 (reversal of affect defense).

2. She complained of pressure in her upper thorax (a displacement of sensation).

3. She avoided the sight of excited men engaged in conversation with women (precautionary avoidance).

4. She did not know where she had learned about sex (amnesia).

5. Her associations tended to be about her father's love affair with Frau K. and her anger at his immorality rather than her own love interest in Herr K. (projection).

Possible instances of direct expression of sexual motivation in the Dora case:

1. She reported that she and a former governess had discussed sex openly and extensively.

2. She shared with Frau K. the secrets of the K.'s marital difficulties.

3. She praised Frau K.'s "adorable white body," etc.

A rough count indicated that the first twenty-six indirect expressions of sex were paralleled by only three direct expressions of sex. The "direct-ness-indirectness ratio" would be 3/26. Presumably with success in therapy there would be a closer balance between the two, and finally a reversal in which indirect expressions would become rarer than direct ones.

Of course the procedure would entail considerable work by experts in collating a representative group of well-chosen examples of what actual practicing analysts in the Freudian tradition would consider to be indirect expressions of impulse (repressive defenses) as compared to direct ones. These would become the basis of a scoring scheme that could be applied to any segment of recorded therapy material.

6. Remoteness Ratios based on Tests.

a. Indirect Tests. Considerable work has been done on the development of indirect estimates of attitude, opinion, and motivation. Some of these have been reviewed by the Maccobys (16). The various methods all ask subjects to talk or to fill out questionnaires about how *other* people feel on certain emotionally sensitive questions. Then the procedure is repeated, this time with the subject asked to indicate how *he* feels. The difference between degree of expression in the two cases constitutes the estimate of unconscious attitude or motive.

The self-reference technique of Hanfmann and Getzels (11) is a good illustration. The subject is asked to fill out quickly a sentence completion test about how *other* people feel, and afterward is required to go over it a second time with instructions to indicate which of the sentences could apply to *him*. One assumes that the original completion of the sentence fragments would correspond to an indirect estimate of impulse, and that those sentences that the subject was willing to accept as true of himself would give an estimate of direct expression of impulse. Of course the sentences would have to be devised in such a way as to provoke material of interest to the Freudian theory.

Self versus social attitude discrepancies furnish other examples. A number of investigators (5, 17, 21) have found that people are willing to express personally unacceptable impulses when these are disguised as items in questionnaires on social attitudes. With Mark's questionnaire (17), for instance, subjects could be asked to indicate how other people rear their children by responding to such statements as "It's all right for a mother to sleep with a child because it gives him a feeling of being loved and wanted." It would be simple to use the double administration technique then and ask subjects how they would rear their own children.

175

b. Projective Test Remoteness Ratios. The projective testing movement of recent decades is based on an extension of Freud's concept of a remoteness gradient to include tests such as the Rorschach and TAT, which are considered to establish conditions comparable to remoteness in dreams, free associations, and fantasy.

These tests offer possibilities for development of test remoteness ratios. One could contrast the amount of impulse expressed under less remote conditions with the amount of impulse expressed under the presumably more remote conditions of responding to the projective material. One ratio might be the proportion of impulse expression in a standard hour of interview in which one related one's life history to that in a standard hour storytelling to TAT cards. The TAT cards have the virtue (for this purpose) of having been selected largely on the basis of Freudian theory.

Tompkins (23) has advanced the hypothesis that *within* a TAT story one can compare the amount of directly and indirectly expressed impulse. For instance the hero may simply say, "He killed this fellow," a direct statement of aggression; or he may introduce greater remoteness in several ways such as placing the event in the distant past: "A long time ago these cave men fought, and he killed this fellow." Tompkins thinks that repression can be estimated from within the TAT by noting how much remoteness is introduced by the storyteller when he expresses dangerous impulses.

OBSERVATIONAL LANGUAGE AND PRIMAL REPRESSION

Since Freud worked with adults in therapy, his theory of primal repression is an inference based upon the childish transference attitudes and behavior discoverable in the memories of adults. One would not expect his writings on childhood repression to be very rich in observational materials. If the concept of primal repression is to be translated into observational language as fruitfully as seems possible with so many of Freud's other concepts, child analysts would have to play a large role in such a translation. Only some first suggestions are possible from Freud's own writings.

Primal Repression in Infancy. This was conceived by Freud as being a response to non-gratification of physical needs:

1. Prior to the need state, the organism was in a state of equilibrium.
2. The result of the ungratified need was a flooding of the organism with stimuli too great to cope with, thus unbalancing the equilibrium.

3. This overstimulated state was a trauma, defined psychologically as a state of overwhelming helplessness.

4. In the force versus antiforce model, this overstimulation had the role of a force which, in later repression, was always an instinctual force.

5. The organism's automatic, innate reaction was to bring about action aimed at restoring the pre-existing equilibrium. It did this because of the innate tendency to keep tension at the lowest level (Conservation principle, Nirvana principle). This resulted in a tendency to reinstate the pre-existing condition, a tendency which, in its general form, Freud called the "repetition-compulsion" principle.

While the formal structure of the theoretical idea may be stated in a clear and consistent way at this very abstract level, this is certainly one place where the lack of an observational language coordinated with the theoretical terms is a definite problem.

From the force side, the observational terms are clear enough in a general way, since Freud pointed explicitly to hunger as an example, and his account clearly suggests physiological needs in general.

The counterforce side is another matter. What would it mean, in observational terms, to say that the infant attempts to get rid of the overtension state and restore the pre-existing one? All one can see is that he cries. Are his screams indicators of trauma and of a repression tendency? It would not be unreasonable to interpret extreme crying as a trauma state, but what shows an attempt at repression? Is it stopping crying, acting as if he weren't hungry, or what? Or is it that the infant, in some sense, tries to stem the tide of overstimulation, and this trying, which fails, is the attempt at repression?

Whatever the nature of the anticathectic force in infantile repression, there is nothing in Freud's writings that I have discovered which would allow one to state it in observational terms.

Primal Repression in Later Childhood. After the period of infantile traumas, Freud said, the child comes to fear absence of the mother, and to experience this absence as a trauma. The same is true, later, for castration threat in the Oedipal period.

1. Separation traumas. Here the existence of a trauma state and fears of such would not be difficult to state in observational terms. The panic of a small child separated from his mother is easily observed, as are his various fears of such separation. A child who fearfully and unreasonably refuses to stay not only with babysitters but even with other siblings or the

177

father, or who insists on having his mother visible at every moment, is an example Freudian child analysts would probably be willing to use in agreeing upon observation-level indicators of separation fears. One could also be reasonably sure of agreement on what they would call a traumatic response to having actually been separated from the mother.

An observation language for the counterforce would be a more difficult though probably a solvable problem. What would constitute an attempt to repress in the case of separation traumas? I expect child analysts could supply the needed answer here. If, for instance, a child whose mother was actually absent kept insisting she was actually at home "somewhere," this denial attempt would no doubt be accepted as a clue to the repression tendency. Little Hans's dream that "I thought you were gone and I had no mummy to coax with" is an example of an expressed fear of separation that even a layman would find acceptable evidence.

2. Castration traumas. The suffering of a castration trauma by a child is probably an unobservable event in itself. Presumably it would be in the nature of a panic state, which is observable enough. If a child in such a panic state said he was afraid of castration, that would be good evidence. But psychoanalysis does not seem to work in terms of such actually observable castration panic states, but, rather, in terms of an anticipatory fear of such. To what extent this may be stated in observational terms is not clear. Little Hans's fear that horses would bite him was interpreted by Freud as a castration fear, but this is *not* observational evidence. It involves accepting the psychoanalytic assumption of the symbolism that "bite" = "castrate." Castration threat would be statable in observational language only insofar as the child directly stated such a fear. In Freud's Little Hans case, there is no such direct statement. Castration fear is inferred, and the inference is based upon further theoretical assumptions.

It would seem, then, that, in principle, castration fear is observable, but in the practice of psychoanalysts it is customarily inferred from evidence that requires theoretical assumptions to translate the manifest language and actions of the child into the unobserved castration fear.

OBSERVATIONAL LANGUAGE AND SUCCESSFUL DEFENSE

Successful defense presents a radically different problem from unsuccessful defense. In the latter there are two motives at work and both the force and counterforce have many observable effects upon behavior. But it is the essence of successful defense that the instinctual force no longer exists, either having been "destroyed in the id," or changed to an acceptable impulse (in sublimation and absorption), or having lost its motivational power (in repudiation). Since there is no instinctual force, there need be no counterforce, so that anticathectic tendencies are also absent.

The situation is not unlike the case of a visitor to a former battleground on which a battle had been fought and victory won by one side (the anticathexis), but on which the struggle had left no traces visible at the present. There would be, in some cases, certain formations present in the landscape (sublimations, absorptions) which some theorists would insist were products of the battle (socially approved motives and character traits) and evidence for it, but which, to the observer's eye, would appear indistinguishable from other natural surroundings he would have expected to see had there been no battle.

Successful defense appears to be a purely theoretical concept in Freud's scheme; there are no observable correlates that would indicate the presence of successful defense.

XI

✗. Conclusions

THE separation of repression and defense by restricting the former to amnesia was, in theory, possible in 1926 when Freud made his half-hearted gesture, and still is — but highly unlikely in practice. There is today the same basic difficulty that prevented Freud from effectively refining the terminological usage that had developed over thirty years: the close association of "repression" with a far broader conceptual meaning than amnesia. As we have seen, "repression" came to be used for alternative manifestations of the central Freudian hypothesis of interplay between instinctual force and anticathectic counterforce. Possibly a consistent and unitary meaning for "repression" could have been established if the term had been used to refer only to the effects of the interaction between force and counterforce on the *one* psychological process of consciousness, as was apparently Freud's intention in the 1915 "Repression" paper. Even then the term would have had to include the repressive defenses and various resistance effects as well as amnesia. But Freud did not thus restrict his use of "repression"; it came to comprehend finally even inhibitions and childhood responses in which the condition of consciousness itself was in doubt. Hence "repression" came to mean virtually any manifestation of the effect of the interplay between force and counterforce upon psychological processes. It was not applied to regression, sublimation, condemnation, and absorption, but except for these, "repression" and "defense" became indistinguishable.

There is no way out of the terminological confusion except that taken in the end by Freud, and, as far as I can tell, by most psychoanalysts since, which is to treat the two words as synonyms for one idea.

180

Note should be made of one very unsatisfactory but widely adopted solution to the problem. Those offering this solution say that repression is a first phase of all defenses, and that particular defenses "complete" what repression does not adequately take care of. This theory acknowledges the inseparability of repression and defense, but it is unsatisfactory because the repression that it posits as a response preceding another defense (such as projection) is not given any meaning. It is a purely hypothetical process, like the negative weight of phlogiston in early chemistry, posited only to solve a conceptual dilemma. What does a person *do* when he represses prior to projecting? Does he forget? inhibit? expel from consciousness? In fact, projection alone is sufficient. By misrepresenting the ownership of objectionable impulses he keeps them away from conscious recognition. There is no separate preceding process of repression that can be either given a theoretical definition or expressed in observable terms.

Before leaving the semantic issue, I should like to offer a classification scheme for the use of terms *within* the theory of repression and defense that may help in clarifying the conceptual distinctions implicit or explicit in Freud's thought. In most cases the terms are Freud's own.

Defense: all forms of ego-protection against dangerous impulses. *Repression*: a general synonym for "defense."

Successful defense: outcomes of the interplay of force and counterforce in which the force (instinct) loses its original motivational impetus and its former anxiety-arousing character. In this category are sublimation, destruction in the id, condemnation, and absorption.

Unsuccessful defense: outcomes of the interplay of force and counterforce in which the force (instinct) actively continues to have its original motivational impetus and its anxiety-arousing character.

1. *Amnesic repression*: unconsciously motivated forgetting.
2. *Repressive defenses*: all defenses whose main mechanism of ego-protection centers around alterations of the conscious representation of motives and associated content. These include amnesia, conversion, displacement, projection, reaction-formation, isolation, undoing, reversal, turning round on the self, and denial. (Amnesic repression is included in this category for most purposes but it should be kept in mind that there is some difference: it alters consciousness by *omission*, whereas the other repressive defenses all misrepresent by *distortion*.)
3. *Inhibition*: mechanisms of ego-protection that achieve control of anxiety by preventing the arousal of feared motives.
   a. *Emotional inhibition*: the direct inner blockage of emotional

181

arousal under conditions normally adequate to instigate the motive in question.

   b. *Ego-restriction*: the inhibition of participation in activities that would arouse the feared motive states.

4. *Regression*: the substitution of an earlier developmental and sex-associated drive for a later and more mature genital sex interest as a means of controlling anxiety. Regression is not primarily either consciousness-altering or inhibitory, although both of these types of protective responses may be secondarily associated with regression.

5. *Primal repression*: all forms of defense prior to the establishment of the superego in the Oedipal period.

   a. *Infantile repression*: the response to tensions arising from non-gratification of physical needs.

   b. *Childhood repression*: responses to the threat of separation from the mother, or to castration threat.

It will be noted that reversal and turning round on the self appear as repressive defenses in the foregoing suggested classification, and that this is inconsistent with their treatment in Chapter II, where they apparently stood in contrast to repressive defenses. This difference derives from my disagreement with Freud in classifying these two defenses. In the 1915 paper on "Repression" Freud separated reversal and turning round on the self from such defenses as displacement, conversion, and reaction-formation, all of which shared a kinship as forms of repression in Freud's discussion. I suggested (in Chapter II) that this kinship could be taken into account best by introducing the covering concept of "repressive defenses," to include displacement, conversion, amnesia, and certain other defenses not specifically mentioned by Freud in his "Repression" paper, but which his earlier treatment had also grouped as "variants of repression."

Freud's reason for separating off reversal and turning round on the self from the other defenses that he called "forms of repression" was that he believed that they were used early in childhood before consciousness was clearly separated from unconsciousness, and, since he was defining repression in terms of rejection from consciousness, he could not include reversal and turning round on the self as falling under his definition.

I feel that, here, Freud's attempt at a classification of defenses became complicated by his assumptions about the age at which consciousness developed, and that it was his theoretical conviction that consciousness and unconsciousness developed in later childhood that determined the separate status given to reversal and turning round on the self. If one chooses not to make Freud's assumption about age, but adheres to the general logic that he seemed to be following in the other main statements he made about repression, these two defenses appear to belong with the other repressive defenses as being ego-protective mechanisms which depend upon a distortion of the conscious representation of impulses as their principal means of controlling anxiety.

In the case of reversal Freud himself actually listed it as a form of repression (repressive defense in my terms) both in his writings before 1915 and in 1926 (see Chapter I). This suggests that his attempt at classification in 1915 was complicated by his assumptions concerning development, and that, when these latter considerations were not entering into his thinking, he grouped reversal with the defenses which I am designating repressive defenses.

These considerations make less comprehensive the argument presented in Chapter II to the effect that Freud himself wrote as if he had implicit in his thinking a concept such as repressive defenses to which he never attached a separate name, but they do not seriously undermine it. The argument still applies with the same force as before to the eight defenses of amnesia, conversion, displacement, projection, reaction-formation, isolation, undoing, and denial, and this fact is certainly sufficient to establish the point. Reversal and turning round on the self are simply more complicated cases. I would group them with the repressive defenses because to do so is consistent with the main logic of Freud's definitions and implicit groupings. It should be recognized, however, that, in 1915 at least, Freud would not have agreed with my suggested classification in the case of these two defenses.

RESEARCH ON REPRESSION AND FREUD'S THEORY

Most research on repression has followed a common pattern. The experimental subjects are engaged in activities that normally leave a residue of recallable memory traces. These subjects may be persons for whom the activities in question already have painful associations due to their past experiences, or a painful emotional state may be aroused in them by artificially created shock, threats, or insults from the experimenter. After being engaged in the activity under conditions of psychic pain, the experimental subjects are tested for recall of events associated with it, and their responses are compared with those of control subjects for whom the same activities were not painful. A lower rate of recall for pained subjects is taken as evidence of repression.

An experiment reported by Zeller (25) is one of the best, and serves well as an example for discussion. Zeller's subjects memorized a list of thirty nonsense syllables, after which they were divided into experimental and control groups. The experimental group members were assigned a block-tapping task that looked easy but became so complex that they were unable to judge their own success in executing it; they were subjected to depreciating remarks about their poor performance and its reflection upon their intelligence. The controls were engaged in similar tasks but no insulting comments were made to them.

Both groups were then tested for recall of the nonsense syllables and the insulted group proved reliably poorer. Several days later the two groups repeated the procedure, but this time those who had been insulted were allowed to succeed and were praised for their performance (in order to "lift" the repression). A new recall test showed that this treatment was accompanied by a reliable increase in recall of the nonsense syllables, though the experimental group was still significantly poorer than the control group.

The failure of recall after insult was interpreted by Zeller as consistent with the theory of repression, and the improvement after praise as proof that the repression had been "lifted," though the experimenter acknowledged that other interpretations were equally plausible.

It should be recognized that experiments such as these are of interest in their own right, quite apart from whether they have any relation to Freud's theory. Since, however, they are inspired by Freudian psychology, and most readers interpret them as evidence for or against Freud's theory, it is important to examine such studies against the background of the extensive review of the original theory presented in this book. Such a consideration suggests several comments and comparisons.

First there is the matter of consciousness. Experimenters who have done research on repression have been hampered by Freud's reluctance to discuss consciousness. He mostly assumed that the reader would understand the meaning of the term without precise definition: "The starting point for this investigation is provided by a fact without parallel, which defies all explanation or description — the fact of consciousness. Nevertheless, if anyone speaks of consciousness, we know immediately and from our own most personal experience what is meant by it." (1940, p. 34.)

But what is to be the experimenter's criterion for whether an event is conscious or not? Is ability to verbalize to be equated with consciousness?

184

What about ideas that are in consciousness but are intentionally suppressed because the person is unwilling to reveal them?

Freud's own view (presented in Chapter VIII) that ideas normally repressed can be conscious providing they are remote from ego recognition, and that repressed thoughts can be conscious in the form of daytime fantasies, is likely to be confusing rather than clarifying. It sounds as though conscious but intentionally withheld ideas may be counted as part of the repressed unconscious. This is not so. The following passages provide the most helpful statements Freud made on this question:

"It is by no means impossible for the product of unconscious activity to pierce into consciousness, but a certain amount of exertion is needed for the task. When we try to do it ourselves, we become aware of a distinct feeling of *repulsion* which must be overcome, and when we produce it in a patient we get the most unquestionable signs of what we call his *resistance* to it. . . . The distinction between foreconscious [preconscious] and unconscious activity is not a primary one, but comes to be established after repulsion has sprung up. Only then the difference between foreconscious ideas, which can appear in consciousness and reappear at any moment, and unconscious ideas which cannot do so gains a theoretical as well as a practical value." (1912a, p. 264.)

"A new turn taken by criticisms of the unconscious deserves consideration at this point. Many investigators, who do not refuse to recognize the facts of psycho-analysis but who are unwilling to accept the unconscious, find a way out of the difficulty in the fact, which no one contests, that in consciousness (regarded as a phenomenon) it is possible to distinguish a great variety of gradations in intensity and clarity. Just as there are ideas which are very vividly, keenly, and definitely conscious, so we also entertain others which are but faintly, hardly even noticeably conscious; those that are most faintly conscious are, it is argued, the ones to which psychoanalysis wishes to apply the unsuitable name unconscious. These, however (the argument proceeds), are also conscious or 'in consciousness' just as much as the others, and can be made fully and intensely conscious if sufficient attention is paid to them.

". . . this attempt to equate what is unnoticed with what is unconscious is obviously made without taking into account the dynamic conditions involved, which were the decisive factors in formulating the psycho-analytic view. For it ignores two facts: first, that it is exceedingly difficult and requires very great effort to concentrate enough attention on

185

something unnoticed of this kind; and secondly, that when this has been achieved the thought which was previously unnoticed is not recognized by consciousness, but often seems utterly alien and opposed to it and is promptly disavowed by it." (1923, footnote to pp. 14–15.)

These statements provide a basis for establishing the criterion for consciousness. It is clear that, when an impulse is in the margins of consciousness (hence remote from ego recognition) but is repressed, the subject cannot verbalize such material for the experimenter. More crucially, it is clear that *the subject cannot perceive it clearly himself*. Such a perception of inner thoughts requires a fixing of attention upon them. In the case of repressed but marginally conscious thoughts, attention *cannot* be fixed upon them in that state. If attention is directed steadily to such a marginal thought, it changes in such a way that its true character is not perceptible to the subject. Finally, the general theory of repression and defense as reviewed herein makes it clear that the motivational basis of the "repression" felt for the marginally conscious ideas has these specific characteristics: anxiety and guilt are involved; the anxiety and guilt are in the nature of anticipatory warnings that a trauma state will occur if the elusive thought is pursued; the defensive turning of attention from the thought is automatic and involuntary, and the person is *unaware* that he has turned from it to something else.

In a study such as Zeller's, the subject is unable to recall the full list of nonsense syllables. Does he consciously know the missing syllables or not? The experimenter has to depend entirely upon verbal report. Freud used verbal failure too, of course, but the therapeutic situation differs from the experimental one in that the therapist is not limited to this first verbal report. After being insulted by the experimenter, the subject may be quite consciously disinclined to cooperate further. This is not repression if he is *aware* of his own uncooperativeness. The experimenter does not go on, as the therapist does, to extensive and minute examination of the state of the subject's consciousness. For the purposes of basic research on repression, however, it is necessary to establish by such intensive qualitative examination not only that there is failure to verbalize, but that there are no conscious motives making for an uncooperative attitude and hence a simple unwillingness to try to recall material. In a sense, of course, the repressing patient is unwilling to try, but this unwillingness is itself unconscious.

Thus, failure to verbalize may be due to a variety of reasons: conscious deception; poor cooperation which the subject is aware of; strong unconscious emotional resistance to attending to material marginally present in consciousness. Only the third of these qualifies as repression. The existence of resistance has to be demonstrated independently of the failure to verbalize.

A second point to be made is that the most obvious difference between the usual research study on repression and repression in the clinic is, of course, the intensity and quality of motives involved.

It is hard to state the degree of intensity of motives involved in clinical repression except by referring to the typically drastic motivational situations of the patient as was done in Chapter VII, where a sample of cases was reviewed. As we saw there (page 120) intensity of motives and of anxiety was considered by Freud to be a definite factor in repression.

Since laboratory analogues that attempt to create their own motive states will always be limited, for ethical reasons, to the use of relatively mild stimuli, negative findings from such studies can never be conclusive. After all, the phenomenon of water boiling cannot be confirmed by any study where temperatures of less than 212° must be used.

The quality of motives involved is of even greater significance. Freud's theory is about the repression of primal motives, or motives having associative connections with primal motives. The primal motives are traumatic experiences of infancy and childhood and panic fears of such traumas. Adult repression in Freud's theory always involved adult sex or hostility having associative connections with these childhood traumas.

It must be kept in mind that, according to Freud's theory, primal traumas and associatively repressed motives involving adult sex and hostility are found only in cases of unsuccessful defense. Normal persons differ from neurotics in that they use mostly successful defenses; they also do use some unsuccessful defense, but Freud does not tell us how much. If one is interested in testing Freud's theory, then, it is obvious that only neurotic patients of the type his theory is about (those with hysteria, phobias, compulsion neuroses, anxiety states) are suitable subjects. They are the only persons for whom the linkages of adult sex and hostility to primal traumas can be assumed to exist. Not only must the subjects be such neurotics, the stimuli used must have associative connections with primal motives. In neuroses, this connection can only be safely assumed for genital sex, more hazardously for hostility. Nonsense syllables just would not do. The most pertinent stimulus to use would undoubtedly be castration threat with neurotic male subjects. The theory is clearest for males and castration threat is clearly stated by Freud to be the most crucial and universal male experience to which neurotics respond with unsuccessful defenses and to which normal persons respond with successful defenses.

In view of these discrepancies between laboratory and clinic, it can only be said of the usual research studies into repression that they involve tests of the *generality* of Freud's theory of repression. While Freud spoke loosely about "mankind's repressions" in his general comments on society in a way that sometimes suggested that we are all repressors, the clinical theory of repression is actually tightly drawn and specific to certain kinds of motives, in certain kinds of adults, who have had certain kinds of childhood experiences. The studies on repression typically test whether Freud was right in insisting upon these restrictions, which, as in the case of sexual content and childhood traumas, he repeatedly held to through all of his writings on repression. If their findings are negative, one can conclude that Freud was correct in having set such restrictions. But, as long as one uses remote analogues, one cannot say from negative results whether the theory itself is correct within the limits Freud set. Positive findings in such analogues show that the theory applies to other kinds of stimuli and other kinds of subjects (normal persons) than Freud specified, proving that Freud was wrong in setting limits to the theory and supporting but not directly proving the theory itself. The possibility would still exist that the theory does not work in the clinical cases using the motivational stimuli to which Freud restricted the theory.

Hence, remote analogues can test some interesting hypotheses that are suggested by Freudian psychology, but cannot be tests of Freud's theory of repression and defense.

MEASURING REPRESSION

According to many critics of psychoanalysis, the reason for its general failure to progress from its original status as a brilliant set of hypotheses to a position of assured scientific standing has been the difficulty of devising measures for any of Freud's concepts. Lindzey has expressed this problem clearly: "To summarize, we have examined the impact of a tremendously influential psychological theory and have found a pronounced deficit in relevant experimental findings that are widely accepted. Moreover, this low incidence of significant and verifiable findings seems largely attributable to the absence of measuring instruments adequate to assess psychoanalytic variables. Thus, if we grant the theory an important status on the contemporary scene, we are forced to concede the central importance of efforts to develop instruments that will permit the theory to be efficiently translated into the world of reality. Until this procedural stage has been satisfactorily negotiated it is impossible to carry out coordinated empirical investigations that can be considered valid reflections of the theory." (15, pp. 14–15.)

Chapter X showed that many aspects of the theory of repression can be expressed in an observational language. In principle, any concept for which such correspondence rules for linking it to real events can be stated lends itself to eventual measurement. If the observational statements in Chapter X are correct, there is no doubt that repression is measurable in principle, if not presently in fact (due to lack of the necessary techniques).

The many studies of repression by experimental psychologists, while usually presented as tests of Freud's theory, are also, of course, attempts to measure repression. In Zeller's study, for instance, the number of the thirty nonsense syllables forgotten by the insulted group as compared to the control subjects would be a quantitative indicator of repression tendency if one is willing to extend repression to such situations so remote from the theory.

In my opinion, the reason for the general failure to measure repression tendency has been the general lack of attention to the theory of repression. This book aims to focus attention on the theory, and this chapter and the chapters on the theoretical and observational language of repression and defense are in the nature of a prelude for future attempts at measurement. A few measures are actually suggested in these chapters purely by way of example. The large task of research and development in translating the analysis of observational language presented in Chapter X into actual measures would take the resources of a trained staff working over a period of years. But there is simply no doubt that many, though not all, aspects of repression are measurable.

The most important recommendation to those concerned with developing measurement techniques is that they work with the therapeutic situation. The theory of repression began with observations in therapy and is most fundamentally a hypothetical construction made in an attempt to account for the phenomena of therapy. As shown earlier, Freud's writings are richest in their treatment of repression and defense in relation to therapeutic phenomena. He pointed explicitly not only to different types of resistance indicators but also to many specific subtypes, and gave numerous actual examples of most of these. Repression-resistance as a type of indicator was particularly singled out. Transference resistance, too, is clearly measurable. Some of the studies referred to in Chapter X are already using measures that need only be given a suitable Freudian content in order for them to constitute adequate measures of transference distortion.

As Chapter X showed, not all segments of the theory of repression are statable in an observational language. The parts that are not cannot be measured. Among these are infantile repression, castration traumas, and expressions of impulses in dreams. One cannot say what the observational language for "to repress" would be in the case of infants responding repressively to traumas that come from non-gratification of physical needs. Castration traumas, in principle, are statable in observation language. But I am not sure this is ever possible in practice. An observation language would require the child to be in a panic, and the panicked child to reveal, in direct terms, that he feared castration. It is my impression that analysts in practice do what Freud did when he equated Little Hans's fear of horses biting him with fear of castration. This is a Freudian *assumption* and does not qualify as *observation*. Insofar as analysts *only* infer the Oedipus complex on such a symbolic basis, it is not statable in observational terms, and, consequently, not measurable even in principle. There is the same problem with expressions of impulses in dreams. If a dream can be shown to express repressed impulses only by making further Freudian assumptions, the concept of dream remoteness cannot be stated in observational terms and therefore one cannot use dreams in measuring repression.

Other aspects of the theory also, of course, may not be measurable. If repressed impulses, for example, do not express themselves openly in free association, but require Freudian translation rules to show that free associations contain repressed impulses, one cannot use free-association data either.

It is my own belief that these limitations are not a serious problem except for the measurer who might want to work with repression literally in terms of the sex theory. The bothersome translation rules in Freud (best seen in the "dreamwork" mechanisms like symbolism, condensation, and omissions), in my opinion, exist only as means of maintaining

Freud's dogmatic belief that all manifest motives refer, in some ultimate sense, to sex. The sexual character of manifest motives is simply not a principle that can be stated in an observational language, since their "sexual" nature can only be established by employing the translation rules which are themselves theoretical assumptions. Any part of the theory where this is a problem is outside the bounds of measurement.

But if we thus dismiss Freud's dogmatism about sex, does this not invalidate the argument of the last section that research on repression should involve sexual stimuli? I do not feel it does because I believe that actual sex (not symbolic sex) was involved in many of Freud's clinical cases, and especially in those that suggested the theory of repression to him. The theory might be true for these defining cases involving real sex and not be true for other cases without manifest sexual content to which Freud generalized the theory by means of his various translation rules.

Sex *is* treated quite differently from other motives in child training. In their relations with children adults treat sex in ways that may lead the child to imagine all sorts of untrue things about it (such as castration). We avoid talk about sex and sex actions with children. Possibly, because of this special character of sex as a motive and our unique treatment of sex, the theory of repression may be quite true as it relates to sex for people brought up under particular cultural conditions such as existed in Freud's day, or even today. It may not be true, or may be less true, as it relates to other motives or as it is applied to other child-training conditions.

As a final point on measurement, it should be emphasized that Chapter X on the observational language of repression and defense is *not* meant to treat the measurement problem comprehensively, but only to serve the fundamental prior need of stating the theory in observational terms. Once this is done, measurement is only a practical problem, though an enormous one, of finding suitable techniques for quantification.

Unless one wanted to restrict oneself to measuring repression "as Freud meant it" (it is hard to imagine any research group wanting to do this), it would not be wise to start on actual development of measures until an adequate survey of the best usages since Freud is carried out and a sufficient theoretical and observational statement of these views drawn up and integrated with Freud's in a way satisfying to today's leaders in Freudian psychology. After all, they are the ones who would have to play a principal role, and they would hardly want to spend time developing measures based only upon repression as Freud meant it.

191

MEASURES OF REPRESSION AS ESTIMATES OF ILLNESS AND THERAPEUTIC EFFECTS

In addition to the interest it has for experimental psychologists concerned with the scientific status of Freud's theory, measuring repression is of course one of the most pressing needs in psychotherapy. As long as psychotherapists cannot measure therapeutic effectiveness, they leave themselves open to such critics as Eysenck (8) who has charged that psychoanalytic treatment, as judged by reports of some five psychoanalytic institutes that he reviewed, is worse than no treatment at all. He claimed that 44 per cent of patients treated by psychoanalysis improve, compared to 64 per cent treated by eclectic therapists, and 72 per cent who improve if merely treated by their family physician or given only custodial care.

While it is true that Eysenck cannot prove his charge, it is also true that psychoanalysts, or any therapist today, cannot refute it. To do either requires measures that do not exist. It is a scientific disgrace that we do not have such measures — and, tragically, an unnecessary one.

VALIDATING THE THEORY OF REPRESSION AND DEFENSE

There is still the larger question of the scientific status of the theory of repression and defense. Thus far, only amnesic repression has been studied by experimental psychologists, and this only in the form of very remote laboratory analogues. It might be helpful to look at some problems still to be investigated.

One such problem is the identification of the crucial hypotheses that would have to be tested to validate the theory of repression and defense. At the most general level, there are three such hypotheses: that primal repressions exist in childhood; that adult repression exists; that adult repression and childhood repression are causally related.

The main difficulty one would have in testing these propositions lies in the establishment of childhood repression. The critical test would have to be done with castration trauma. As already indicated, castration trauma is not observable if it is always inferred on a symbolic or other indirect basis that depends in turn upon further theoretical assumptions involved in Freud's various translation rules. If this problem is solvable, the theory is confirmable in principle, though arranging a test would present large practical problems.

Of course there is a real possibility that the theory of repression has

192

CONCLUSIONS

more generality than Freud supposed: that childhood traumas of a non-sexual kind (ones that *are* observable) do take place, that the child responds in inadequate ways to these because of his immaturity, and that, later, as an adult, he tends to use these same primitive kinds of response for adult problems that associatively rearouse the trauma. In fact this more general proposition, implicit in Freud's theory, is a more important one than the particular formulation that Freud gave it. Its testing would involve the same three propositions, but without restriction to sexual motives.

Four other hypotheses to be tested may be singled out here. These are important but of a lesser order than the three basic ones.

1. That repression and defense are response patterns limited to sexual and sex-associated motives. This is challenged by neo-Freudians, of course. The laboratory analogues are to some extent concerned with this proposition.

2. That all the various manifestations of the interplay of force and counterforce pointed to by Freud are indicators of the struggle between instinct and anticathexis.

In the analogy with measurement of temperature posed in Chapter X, it was seen that an *unobservable* phenomenon of increased heat activity is assumed by physicists to be the origin of various manifestations of heat that *are* observable and measurable. The manifestations of heat are of an even greater variety than Freud claimed for repression and defense, including volumetric expansion, color changes, heat sensations, conductivity changes, pressure changes, and many more. It was pointed out that, even in physics, these various manifestations do *not* yield measures of heat energy that agree perfectly. Nevertheless, there *is* considerable agreement between readings, say, on an alcohol thermometer and on a mercury thermometer. The disagreements are of little consequence for most problems.

In the case of the theory of repression, one of the important but implicit hypotheses is that the various manifestations of the interplay of force and antiforce all stem from one general process. Insofar as they do, there ought to be some correlation among measures derived from the five types of resistance, for instance, and measures of resistance ought to have some relation to estimates derived from the other major manifestations specified by Freud, such as repressive defenses, symptoms, remoteness, and inhibition.

193

In point of fact some of these might show zero correlations, and some might show agreement. Other manifestations suggested by post-Freudians. or devised by experimental psychologists, might, on the other hand, agree well with one or two of Freud's manifestations. If so, the theory could be broadened. To the extent that some manifestations do not show correlation with any others, one would have a basis for improving the theory by dropping out noncorrelating manifestations.

3. That there is constant pressure in the action of instincts and anti-cathexis. Freud's insistence that instincts act as uninterrupted forces led in turn to assumption of a constant counterforce in anticathexis.

As was pointed out above, this assumption is in sharp contrast to the tenets of motivational theory in psychology. We usually assume that any motive, even sex, is normally inactive but can be aroused to tension by suitable internal or external stimulation.

Freud's assumption may have been a reasonable one in dealing with patients having strong but inhibited sexual motives in a situation where the patient lay on a couch, particularly if the patient was female (Freud was handsome in his forties) and if continence during therapy, which used to be one of Freud's rules, was required. One can well imagine that sex would act as a constant pressure under such conditions! But these may not be representative conditions from which to generalize about motives.

To me, Freud's assumption of constant pressure seems unlikely as a general conception about motives, but, insofar as conditions of therapy and patients are similar to his, it might be useful in describing the behavior of sexual interest and defense against it *in such situations*.

4. That motives can and inevitably will become conscious if not repressed. Few have noticed this bit of rationalistic psychology in Freud. He seemed to feel that motives would naturally be conscious except for repression. Freud's view on this point stands in sharp contrast to the modern psychologist's assumption of the existence of unconscious motives that are not repressed but still cannot be made conscious by an act of attention. Whether Freud or the modern view is right is an important point that needs to be experimentally established.

In addition to these hypotheses, there are two other problem areas. The study of regression presents a special difficulty. In its literal Freudian meaning, regression is probably an unconfirmable hypothesis. In regression an adult sexual motive is defensively replaced by a pregenital one, and this in turn is repressed by one of the repressive defenses. A typical example is Freud's case of Paul, the obsessional neurotic. Paul's manifest problem was a bizarre compulsion to repay a certain officer some money which, in fact, he never owed him, and knew he never owed him. In his analysis Freud demonstrated that the compulsion was the distorted conscious representation of repressed hostility toward the father. But the hostility was not the basic motive, Freud said; rather it was a regressive replacement of the sexual motive, which was the real motive.

The problem here is the same one encountered earlier with castration trauma and dreams, namely, that in order to show that hostility is actually linked to sex, one has to employ Freudian translation rules. Regression, it appears to me, represents a hypothesis that cannot be stated in an observational language insofar as it insists that the first level of repressed motive is a symbolic expression of another, and final, sexual motive.

"Resistance due to the unconscious" has an interesting theoretical status. Freud seems to have postulated the existence of such resistance on the basis of the fact that some patients do not get well. Unconscious guilt and need for self-punishment in "resistance from a sense of guilt" was one explanation he gave for the failure to get well, and a not unreasonable one. But in "resistance due to the unconscious," Freud seems to postulate a purely hypothetical construction in the form of such ideas as "loss of plasticity," the tendency of psychic processes to repeat, and the tendency of the already repressed unconscious to act like a magnet and pull back on processes the analyst is trying to make conscious. Freud does not give an observational correlate of these processes other than the fact of the patient's failure to improve, which was the original empirical problem the concepts were offered in explanation of. The ideas could be developed in observational terms, but this is one of those points where Freud seems to have begun on a suggestive line of thought that he never developed.

My own final conclusion about the confirmability of Freud's theory of repression and defense is that it depends upon how one responds to the problem introduced by Freud's early decision to stick to sex as the mainspring of his general theory of psychology, which led to the greatly expanded use of "translation rules" (symbolism, omissions, condensation, etc., originally described by Freud as the mechanisms of the dreamwork). The fact that, at any point where the translation rules have to be used, Freud's theory becomes unstatable in an observational language has discouraged scientific interest in the theory and has led to widespread charges that it is inherently unconfirmable.

I believe that one has to distinguish between real sex, which is a motivation that is statable in an observation language, and translation-rule sex, which is not.

I believe that Freud's theory of repression and defense was actually worked out largely on the basis of *real sex* and other *real motives*, which were treated by Freud as translation-rule sex. Insofar as this is true, and I believe it to be mainly so, much of Freud's theory of repression and defense not only is confirmable in principle, but can be made testable in fact.

REFERENCES AND INDEX

✶ References to Freud's Writings

THE abbreviation *C.P.* refers to Freud's *Collected Papers*, and *S.E.* to the Standard Edition of Freud's works, both published by the Hogarth Press of London. The first date listed is the original publication date of the article or book.

1893. A case of successful treatment by hypnotism. *C.P.*, V. London: Hogarth, 1950.

1894. The defense neuropsychoses. *C.P.*, I. London: Hogarth, 1950.

1895. Studies on hysteria. With Joseph Breuer. *S.E.*, II. London: Hogarth, 1955.

1896. Further remarks on the defense neuro-psychoses. *C.P.*, I. London: Hogarth, 1950.

1900. The interpretation of dreams. *S.E.*, IV, V. London: Hogarth, 1953.

1905a. Three essays on the theory of sexuality. *S.E.*, VII. London: Hogarth, 1953.

1905b. Fragment of an analysis of a case of hysteria. *S.E.*, VII. London: Hogarth, 1953.

1906. My views on the part played by sexuality in the aetiology of the neuroses. *S.E.*, VII. London: Hogarth, 1953.

1907. Delusion and dreams in Jensen's "Gravida." *S.E.*, IX. London: Hogarth, 1959.

1909. Notes upon a case of obsessional neurosis. *S.E.*, X. London: Hogarth, 1955.

1910. The psychoanalytic view of psychogenic disturbances of vision. *S.E.*, XI. London: Hogarth, 1957.

1911. Psychoanalytic notes on an autobiographical account of a case of paranoia (Dementia Paranoides). *S.E.*, XII. London: Hogarth, 1958.

1912a. The dynamics of transference. *S.E.*, XII. London: Hogarth, 1958.

1912b. A note on the unconscious in psychoanalysis. *S.E.*, XII. London: Hogarth, 1958.

1913. The disposition to obsessional neurosis. *S.E.*, XII. London: Hogarth, 1958.

1914a. On the history of the psychoanalytic movement. *S.E.*, XIV. London: Hogarth, 1957.

1914b. On narcissism: an introduction. *S.E.*, XIV. London: Hogarth, 1957.

1915a. Instincts and their vicissitudes. *S.E.*, XIV. London: Hogarth, 1957.

1915b. Repression. *S.E.*, XIV. London: Hogarth, 1957.

1915c. The unconscious. *S.E.*, XIV. London: Hogarth, 1957.

1915d. Observations on transference-love (Further recommendations on the technique of psycho-analysis, III). *S.E.*, XII. London: Hogarth, 1958.

1916–17. *A general introduction to psychoanalysis.* Garden City, N.Y.: Garden City Publishing Company, 1943. (Published in England as *Introductory lectures on psychoanalysis.* London: Allen and Unwin.)

199

1917. A metapsychological supplement to the theory of dreams. *S.E.*, XIV. London: Hogarth, 1957.
1920. Beyond the pleasure principle. *S.E.*, XVIII. London: Hogarth, 1955.
1921. Group psychology and the analysis of the ego. *S.E.*, XVIII. London: Hogarth, 1955.
1922. Two encyclopedia articles. *S.E.*, XVIII. London: Hogarth, 1955.
1923. *The ego and the id*. London: Hogarth, 1949.
1924. The passing of the Oedipus complex. *C.P.*, II. London: Hogarth, 1950.
1925a. Negation. *C.P.*, V. London: Hogarth, 1950.
1925b. An autobiographical study. *S.E.*, XX. London: Hogarth, 1959.
1926a. Inhibitions, symptoms and anxiety. *S.E.*, XX. London: Hogarth, 1959.
1926b. *The problem of anxiety*. New York: Norton, 1936.
1927. Fetishism. *C.P.*, V. London: Hogarth, 1950.
1930. *Civilization and its discontents*. London: Hogarth, 1955.
1933. *New introductory lectures on psychoanalysis*. New York: Norton, 1933.
1936. A disturbance of memory on the Acropolis. *C.P.*, V. London: Hogarth, 1950.
1937. Analysis terminable and interminable. *C.P.*, V. London: Hogarth, 1950.
1939. *Moses and monotheism*. New York: Knopf, 1939. (Also published by Vintage Books, New York, 1955.)
1940. *An outline of psychoanalysis*. New York: Norton, 1940.
1954. *The origins of psychoanalysis*. New York: Basic Books, 1954.

⅄ References to Works of Other Authors

1. Blake, R. R., and G. V. Ramsey, eds. *Perception, an approach to personality.* New York: Ronald Press, 1950.
2. Blum, G. S. An experimental reunion of psychoanalytic theory with personality vigilance and defense. *Journal of Abnormal and Social Psychology*, 1954, 49, 94–98.
3. Blum, G. S. Perceptual defense revisited. *Journal of Abnormal and Social Psychology*, 1955, 51, 24–29.
4. Brenner, C. The nature and development of the concept of repression in Freud's writings. Pp. 19–46 in *The psychoanalytic study of the child*, Vol. XII. 1957.
5. Campbell, D. T. The indirect assessment of social attitudes. *Psychological Bulletin*, 1950, 47, 15–38.
6. Carnap, R. The methodological character of theoretical concepts. In Feigl and Scriven, eds., *Minnesota studies in the philosophy of science*, Vol. I.
7. Eysenck, H. J. *Dimensions of personality.* London: Routledge and Kegan Paul, 1947.
8. Eysenck, H. J. The effects of psychotherapy: an evaluation. *Journal of Consulting Psychology*, 1952, 16, 319–31.
9. Feigl, H., and M. Scriven, eds. *Minnesota studies in the philosophy of science*, Vol. I: *The foundations of science and the concepts of psychology and psychoanalysis.* Feigl, Scriven, and Grover Maxwell, eds., Vol. II: *Concepts, theories, and the mind-body problem.* Minneapolis: University of Minnesota Press, 1956, 1958.
10. Gough, H. C., and R. F. Suczek. The adjective check-list as a personality assessment research technique. Unpublished manuscript, 1954. Available at Institute of Personality Assessment and Research, 2240 Piedmont Ave., Berkeley, Calif.
11. Hanfmann, Eugenia, and J. W. Getzels. Studies of the sentence completion test. *Journal of Projective Techniques*, 1953, 17, 280–94.
12. Hartmann, Heinz. Psychoanalysis as a scientific theory. Pp. 3–38 in Hook, *Psychoanalysis, scientific method, and philosophy.*
13. Hook, Sidney, ed. *Psychoanalysis, scientific method, and philosophy.* New York: New York University Press, 1959.
14. Levy, Harry B. A critique of the theory of sublimation. *Psychiatry*, 1939, 2, 239–70.
15. Lindzey, G. The assessment of human motives. In G. Lindzey, ed., *The assessment of human motives*, New York: Grove Press, 1960.
16. Maccoby, E. E., and N. Maccoby. The interview: a tool of social science. Pp.

449–97 in Vol. I of G. Lindzey, *Handbook of social psychology*. Cambridge, Mass.: Addison-Wesley, 1954.

17. Mark, J. C. The attitudes of male schizophrenics toward child behavior. *Journal of Abnormal and Social Psychology*, 1953, 48, 185–89.
18. Mowrer, O. H., *et al. Psychotherapy, theory and research*. New York: Ronald Press, 1953.
19. Nagel, E. Methodological issues in psychoanalytic theory. Pp. 38–56 in Hook, *Psychoanalysis, scientific method, and philosophy*.
20. Rogers, C., and Rosalie Dymond, eds. *Psychotherapy and personality change*. Chicago: University of Chicago Press, 1954.
21. Shoben, E. J., Jr. The assessment of parental attitudes in relation to child adjustment. *Genetic Psychology Monographs*, 1949, 39, 101–48.
22. Stephenson, William. *The study of behavior, Q-technique and its methodology*. Chicago: University of Chicago Press, 1953.
23. Tompkins, S. *The thematic apperception test*. New York: Grune and Stratton, 1949.
24. Wallen, R. Food aversions of normal and neurotic males. *Journal of Abnormal and Social Psychology*, 1945, 40, 77–81.
25. Zeller, A. F. An experimental analogue of repression. III. The effects of induced failure and success on memory measured by recall. *Journal of Experimental Psychology*, 1951, 42, 32–38.

✂. Index

203

Test remoteness, 175–76
Three Essays on the Theory of Sexuality, 34, 77, 82, 85, 87, 103, 123
Tompkins, S., 176
Transference, interpreted as resistance, 55–61
Transference resistance: as one of five types of resistance, 55–61; behavioral indicators of, 159–61
Turning round on self, 32

Unconscious, resistance of: as one of five types of resistance, 63–67; behavioral indicators of, 163
Undoing, 23–24
Unsuccessful defenses: theoretical language of, 148–51; suggested definition of, 181

Validation of theory of repression and defense, 192–96
Vicissitudes, relation to repression, 32

Zeller, A. F., 184, 186, 189